the Cake Book

BY CUPCAKE JEMMA

PENGUIN BOOKS

HI GUYS,
JAMIE HERE!

Well, have I got a treat for you, and it comes in the form of the lovely, luscious, super-talented Jemma Wilson, who I had the pleasure of meeting many years ago when she was running a stall at one of my street festivals. Jemma runs a bakery called Crumbs & Doilies, and there's no doubt about it, she's a real pro-baker – the quality of her cakes and bakes is off the chart. They're ridiculously, heart-stoppingly good, and she's great at telling us, in her friendly, direct way, exactly how to make them – from those essential, back-to-basics recipes, to show-stoppers that you won't believe you've made, plus those all-important secrets, hints and tips that'll give you the confidence to cook these amazing creations yourself at home.

This little book is one of the first in a collection of no-nonsense, beautiful cookbooks, inspired by the incredible cooks, chefs and artisans on my Food Tube channel. If you don't know the channel already, hunt us out on YouTube, where myself and a bunch of super-talented people, including Jemma, are uploading exclusive videos every week, with plenty of clever tips, tricks and methods that'll transform your cooking. We're a community of food lovers and experts, who simply want to share our passion with you guys, so if you have any questions, please leave a comment and we'll be happy to answer.

In this little book, Jemma has focused on great cakes and bakes, split up seasonally so you'll have a wonderfully naughty treat to choose from whatever the time of year. It might be small, but it's crammed full of brilliant recipes that'll serve you very well for many years to come. Take it away, Jemma!

Big love,

youtube.com/jamieoliver

Cupcake Jemma

I've always been a creative type. At school art was my favourite subject, and I went on to Camberwell College of Arts to study graphic design, but I was lost there – I couldn't seem to get my teeth into anything, and dropped out after my second year, fully believing that I'd lost my imagination! It wasn't until I discovered baking and set up Crumbs & Doilies that I realized I'd found my creative outlet. It wasn't painting or typography; but it was art, of sorts.

I was a latecomer to baking. Sure, I'd baked a bit as a kid, but I was far more interested in eating cake than in figuring out how to make it. I used to watch my grandma baking, but it didn't occur to me until I grew up just how magical and cool it was that she instinctively measured her ingredients without scales and yet still managed to make perfect, delicious cakes every time.

My own first venture into baking land was in Australia. I'd been staying with my best friend Marisa in Sydney and wanted to host a tea party to say goodbye – it seemed like the British thing to do! I borrowed a recipe book, bought ingredients, then mixed, whipped and beat until my arms were sore. I produced some of the most inedible scones of all time, but other things came out perfectly, and to be honest, it was actually that process of turning some simple ingredients into something delicious which inspired me to carry on when I returned home. I wish I could say I was a natural baker, but I wasn't; still, what I lacked in ability, I made up for in enthusiasm! If a recipe didn't work the first time, I was positive that if I tweaked something here or there, I could improve the result.

I'm certainly not an expert; I'm completely self-taught. I don't know how to make fancy French pastries or confectionery, and I've made plenty of mistakes while trying to figure things out, but I strongly believe that anything is possible if you try hard enough. There's a science to baking, of course, but it's not rocket science! Patience, determination, a willingness to keep trying and the ability to get right back on to my vanilla-sponge horse after I'd fallen off its under-risen back were the only qualities I needed to become a successful baker.

So this book is a collection of some of my favourite recipes, both from my own brain and also from the collective brain of Crumbs & Doilies. Every cupcake recipe makes 24 cakes, because I want you to share – get out there and make friends via cake! The way cakes look and taste can really remind me of the different seasons, so while the first chapter covers baking basics and all the bits and bobs that'll make your cakes extra-special, I've split the remaining chapters up by season – not necessarily because they use seasonal ingredients, but because they evoke that unique feeling that comes with that particular time of year. Nothing here is too complicated, so you've got no excuse not to try them all. One thing we like to do at C&D is to mix up the flavours, so once you've had a go at a few recipes, shuffle things around – put Earl Grey buttercream on your chocolate cupcakes – go nuts! If at first you don't succeed, try, try and try again. And don't forget to check out my videos on Jamie Oliver's Food Tube channel for lots of extra tips and techniques. Enjoy!

Contents

The basics

Spring

Summer

Autumn

Winter

Crumbs & Doilies

I'd been a bartender for almost eight years when it suddenly dawned on me that I should be baking full-time for a living instead. My boss at the time told me about a job opening at Rose Bakery in Dover Street Market, the iconic concept store of Comme des Garçons in Mayfair. I went for it and was amazed to actually get it.

It was at Rose Bakery, working under Rose Carrarini and Junya Yamasaki, that I gained and developed a huge respect for food. I loved working in a small team, using artisanal methods and the highest-quality ingredients, and I learned a huge amount. Nevertheless, a year went by and, despite the fact that I loved my job, I felt it was time to fly the coop, so I took a leap of faith and handed in my notice. Two weeks later I got my first market stall at Sunday UpMarket in Shoreditch; Crumbs & Doilies was born, and I began the most life-changing and exciting journey of my life.

Thankfully, the stall was a huge success. Although I'd started Crumbs & Doilies with no business training, no financial investment and no clue as to where it would go, there were only about four or five other cupcake companies in London at the time, and people were excited. I began taking orders and making cupcakes for weddings and parties, and before I knew it, Crumbs & Doilies was a full time job: I was the baker, the decorator, the delivery guy and the market trader. With the help of my friend and business partner, Sam, who quit his job to work with me full-time, Crumbs & Doilies continued to grow. We moved out of our increasingly cramped flat and into a bigger space with more ovens, more mixers and more team members. It was the biggest and scariest thing we've ever done, but at the same time, definitely the best decision we've ever made. We now have a beautiful, big old kitchen, with the space and facilities to churn out a tonne of cakes every day. I've kept with the early principles I learnt at Rose Bakery: we still use the finest ingredients and we still make everything in small batches, as if I were still baking at home in my mum's kitchen. I've had successes and I've made many, many mistakes, but for me, the most important thing is the quality of the cakes – we've learnt a lot as a team, we never scrimp on our ingredients and we never give up improving our recipes. We are a family.

Hints & tips

DECORATING

I've always preferred to decorate my cupcakes by hand, using a palette knife, a spoon or a spoonula, because I like having more cake than icing! Rather than spreading the icing, I blob it on by bouncing my spoon against the cake – that way it doesn't look too perfect. In some recipes I suggest using a piping bag and nozzle, simply because the cakes look fun when decorated this way, but just do what feels, looks and tastes right to you.

PAPER CASES

Look for cases that are wide enough to fit snugly into a standard-sized muffin tray and are only slightly taller than the muffin holes. They're available at most supermarkets, but if you can only find slightly larger cases, use your instincts and add just a little more cake mixture to each and cook for a bit longer – you might come up a few cupcakes short though!

EQUIPMENT

When it comes to electric mixers, I prefer to use a free-standing type. It'll give you the best results, with the least amount of effort – and I must say, it'll change your baking life! It is quite an investment though, so if you don't have one and you're not quite ready to take the plunge, a hand-mixer will work well too, and they're fairly cheap to buy. If you haven't got either, you can use a good old wooden spoon, but you'll definitely need stamina, muscles and lots of time.

When decorating layer cakes, I recommend investing in a turntable to help you apply the icing evenly. A few different palette knives are really handy too – I've got a 15cm and a 20cm straight palette knife for decorating big and small cakes, as well as a cranked palette knife, which is great for icing the top of a cake without getting your hands in the mixture. I really recommend investing in both small and large piping bags, with different-sized nozzles for decorating and filling cupcakes, and a flexible rubber spatula too, so you never waste that last bit of mixture or icing.

EGGS

I only ever use organic free-range eggs. It's the right thing to do for the happiness of chickens, and they produce a tastier cake. FACT! A pale, flavourless battery egg will produce equally flavourless cakes.

• •

BUTTER

I recommend buying good-quality unsalted butter – any will do, but I prefer Lescure unsalted French butter. It's incredibly good quality and has a really low water content, making it perfect for baking (the tiniest bit of extra fat will keep your cakes moist and squishy for longer). When softening butter, I leave it in a warm place overnight so it's super-spreadable but still holds its shape. If it's too hard, you'll overwork the mixture and end up with dry cakes.

• •

OVEN TEMPERATURES

The temperatures in this book refer to a fan-assisted oven. Even the best ovens can vary, so invest in an oven thermometer to make sure it's just right. If your cupcakes are a bit pointy, the chances are your oven is a little too hot and they've risen too fast, or if your cupcakes are sinking, it might be that your oven isn't hot enough – try adjusting the temperature by a couple of degrees next time.

STORING YOUR CAKES

Cakes are at their best on the day they're baked, but if you're not planning on eating them immediately, store them in an airtight container once they're completely cool and most of them will keep for up to three days at room temperature.

STORING YOUR ICING

If making icing in advance, or if you have some left over, you can store it in an airtight container at room temperature for up to five days. You can also store it in the fridge for up to a week – just make sure you bring it up to room temperature and give it a quick mix before using.

the basics

A few absolute must-knows for your repertoire.

Vanilla cupcakes, vanilla buttercream icing

MAKES 24

TOTAL TIME: 45 MINUTES
PLUS COOLING

FOR THE VANILLA CUPCAKES

250g self-raising flour

250g caster sugar

½ teaspoon bicarbonate of soda

250g unsalted butter, softened

4 large free-range eggs

½ teaspoon vanilla extract

3 tablespoons whole milk

FOR THE VANILLA
BUTTERCREAM ICING

300g unsalted butter, softened

¼ teaspoon vanilla extract

4 tablespoons whole milk

675g icing sugar

YOU NEED

2 x 12-hole muffin trays,
with snug-fitting paper cases

FOR THE VANILLA CUPCAKES

Preheat the oven to 170°C fan/375°F/gas 5. Sift the dry cupcake ingredients into a large bowl, add the butter and eggs, then beat for 60 seconds with an electric mixer (I prefer the free-standing type). Stir the vanilla extract into the milk, then add to the mix and beat for 20 seconds, or until well combined. Scrape down the sides of the bowl with a spatula, then give the mix a final blast for 30 seconds to make sure it's all incorporated. Fill the paper cases two-thirds full with mixture, but don't bother to smooth it out. Bake for 20 minutes, or until they spring back when touched. Leave to cool, transferring to a wire cooling rack after 5 minutes.

FOR THE VANILLA BUTTERCREAM ICING

Beat the butter with an electric mixer for 4 to 5 minutes, or until pale and smooth. Stir the vanilla extract into the milk and set aside. Sift the icing sugar into a large bowl, then add to the butter in two stages, beating well between each. Gradually add the vanilla milk and beat for a further 3 to 5 minutes, or until almost white. Scrape down the sides of the bowl, give it one last blast to gather those neglected bits and you're done.

Once the cupcakes are cool, decorate them with the icing however you like – by hand or using a piping bag and nozzle – and enjoy.

> When filling the paper cases, I like to scoop the mix up with a tablespoon and scrape it off with a teaspoon.

Really easy chocolate cupcakes, chocolate buttercream icing

MAKES 24

TOTAL TIME: 45 MINUTES
PLUS COOLING

FOR THE CHOCOLATE CUPCAKES

150g dark chocolate (70%)

350g plain flour

60g cocoa powder

370g caster sugar

1 teaspoon bicarbonate of soda

3 large free-range eggs

240ml coffee, cooled (see tip below)

240ml buttermilk

210ml vegetable oil

FOR THE CHOCOLATE BUTTERCREAM ICING

180g dark chocolate (70%)

300g unsalted butter, softened

540g icing sugar

4 tablespoons whole milk

YOU NEED

2 x 12-hole muffin trays, with snug-fitting paper cases

FOR THE CHOCOLATE CUPCAKES

Preheat the oven to 160°C fan/350°F/gas 4. Finely chop the chocolate (this is best done in a food processor), then tip into a large bowl and stir in the dry cupcake ingredients and ½ a teaspoon of fine sea salt. Whisk the wet cupcake ingredients together in a separate bowl with an electric mixer (I prefer the free-standing type), then gradually add to the dry mix, whisking until silky smooth. Transfer the mixture to a small jug (you'll need to do this in batches), and carefully fill the paper cases just over two-thirds full. Bake for 20 minutes, or until they spring back when touched. Leave to cool, transferring to a wire cooling rack after 5 minutes.

FOR THE CHOCOLATE BUTTERCREAM ICING

Melt the chocolate in a heatproof bowl over a pan of simmering water, making sure the base doesn't touch the water, then leave to cool for 5 to 10 minutes – the bowl should be just cool enough to handle. Meanwhile, beat the butter with an electric mixer for 4 to 5 minutes, or until pale and smooth. Sift the icing sugar into a large bowl, then add to the butter in two stages, beating well between each. Gradually add the milk and beat for a further 5 minutes, or until well combined. Pour in the melted chocolate bit by bit, mixing as you go, then beat for a couple of minutes, or until the icing is a rich, even chocolate-brown colour. Once the cupcakes are cool, decorate them with the icing and enjoy.

If you don't have freshly brewed coffee, simply mix 1 tablespoon of instant coffee granules with 240ml of hot water instead.

Red velvet cupcakes, cream cheese icing

MAKES
24

TOTAL TIME: 45 MINUTES
PLUS COOLING

FOR THE RED VELVET CUPCAKES

235g self-raising flour

1 tablespoon cocoa powder

250g caster sugar

¾ teaspoon bicarbonate of soda

270g unsalted butter, softened

4 large free-range eggs

3 tablespoons buttermilk

1 teaspoon vanilla extract

½ teaspoon red
food-colouring paste

1½ teaspoons cider vinegar

FOR THE CREAM CHEESE ICING

150g unsalted butter, softened

240g cream cheese

840g icing sugar

YOU NEED

2 x 12-hole muffin trays,
with snug-fitting paper cases

FOR THE RED VELVET CUPCAKES

Preheat the oven to 170°C fan/375°F/gas 5. Sift the dry cupcake ingredients (apart from the bicarbonate of soda) and ¾ of a teaspoon of fine sea salt into a large bowl, add the butter and eggs, then beat for 60 seconds with an electric mixer (I prefer the free-standing type). Mix the buttermilk, vanilla extract and colouring paste in a small jug, then add to the mixture and beat for another 20 seconds, or until well combined. Scrape down the sides of the bowl with a spatula, then give the mix a final blast for a few seconds to make sure it's all incorporated.

In a cup, mix the bicarbonate of soda with the vinegar – as soon as you do this, it'll start to fizz. Working quickly, pour the bubbling mixture into the cake mix and whisk very briefly to incorporate. Give the batter a final mix by hand, then fill the paper cases two-thirds full with mixture, but don't bother to smooth it out. Bake for 20 minutes, or until they spring back when touched. Leave to cool, transferring to a wire cooling rack after 5 minutes.

FOR THE CREAM CHEESE ICING

Beat the butter and cream cheese with an electric mixer for 2 to 3 minutes, or until pale and smooth. Sift the icing sugar into a large bowl, then add to the butter mixture in two stages, beating well between each until beautifully smooth – if the mix seems too loose, add a little more icing sugar until the consistency is just right. Once the cupcakes are cool, decorate them with the icing and a few of your favourite sprinkles and enjoy.

Cream cheese icing is best used straight away, but you can keep it for up to a week in the fridge – just remember to let it come up to room temperature before using.

Chocolate ganache

MAKES 800ML

TOTAL TIME: 10 MINUTES
PLUS COOLING

400g dark chocolate (70%)

450ml double cream

OPTIONAL: FOR CHOCOLATE
ORANGE GANACHE

zest from 1 unwaxed orange

Roughly chop the chocolate and place in a bowl. Gently heat the cream and orange zest (if using) in a small pan over a medium heat until small bubbles start to appear on the surface. Pour it over the chocolate and leave for 1 minute without stirring, then mix gently until smooth. Leave aside to cool for around 1 hour, or until the ganache is a nice, spreadable consistency – if it's still a little loose, place in the fridge for another 15 to 20 minutes, stirring every 5 minutes or so until it's just right. This is the perfect icing for giving your cakes a bit of class. Rich, silky and glossy – it's irresistibly fancy, yet a complete doddle to make.

Play around with flavours if you're feeling adventurous – for added fragrance, I like to add an Earl Grey teabag to the cream as it heats up (just remember to remove it before mixing with the chocolate). You could also try cloves, cardamom pods, a cinnamon stick, a vanilla pod or even a chilli – have a play and see what you come up with!

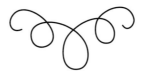

Meringues

MAKES 12

TOTAL TIME: 1 HOUR
PLUS COOLING

white wine vinegar or
fresh lemon juice

4 large free-range egg whites

½ teaspoon vanilla extract

250g caster sugar

Store any leftover egg yolks
in a sealable sandwich bag
in the fridge – they're great
for making lemon curd.

Preheat the oven to 170°C fan/375°F/gas 5 and line two 25cm x 35cm baking trays with greaseproof paper. Fat and grease are the sworn enemies of light, fluffy meringues, so wipe your electric mixer (I prefer the free-standing type) with a little vinegar or lemon juice before you start to ensure it's free of them, otherwise your egg whites won't fluff up properly.

Put the egg whites into a large bowl, making sure no stray bits of yolk accidentally sneak in. Add a pinch of fine sea salt and whisk until firm (but not stiff) peaks form. Next add the vanilla extract, then the sugar, one big spoonful at a time, whisking continuously until smooth, silky and stiff peaks form – you'll know it's right when you can rub a little of the meringue mixture between your thumb and forefinger without feeling any sugar granules.

Dot each corner of the greaseproof paper with a small blob of meringue mixture, then turn it over and stick it to the trays. Spoon or pipe the mixture onto the paper so that you end up with 12 equal tennis ball-sized portions. Place in the hot oven and immediately reduce the temperature to 150°C fan/325°F/gas 3. Bake for 40 minutes, then turn the oven off, but don't open the door. Leave the meringues in the oven to cool completely for at least 1 hour – this slow cooking and cooling process is the secret to deliciously chewy meringues.

Remove from the oven and try one (you've earned it!), then store the rest in an airtight container for up to a week. Crumble and use in icing or on desserts, with fresh fruit or in anything else that will benefit from some light, crispy, chewy, meringuey goodness.

Marshmallowy meringue icing

MAKES 350g

TOTAL TIME: 15 MINUTES

3 large free-range egg whites

260g caster sugar

7 tablespoons golden syrup

½ teaspoon cream of tartar

1 teaspoon vanilla extract

YOU NEED

optional: 1 x blowtorch

Combine the egg whites, sugar, golden syrup, cream of tartar, ¼ teaspoon of fine sea salt and 2 tablespoons of cold water in a heatproof bowl. Place the bowl over a pan of simmering water, making sure the base doesn't touch the water, then beat with an electric hand-whisk for around 5 minutes, or until stiff peaks form – you'll know it's right when you can rub a little of the icing mixture between your thumb and forefinger without feeling any sugar granules.

Remove the bowl from the heat, then add the vanilla extract and beat for a further minute, or until light and fluffy. This icing is best used straight away, but you can store it in the fridge for up to 2 days – just bring it up to room temperature before using.

This is a super-cute topping for almost any cake, especially the **bonfire cupcakes** (see page 98) and **super-lemony meringue cake** (see page 70). If you feel like upping the ante, ice your cakes and pop under a preheated grill or blast briefly with a blowtorch for a toasted meringue finish.

Salted caramel

MAKES 300ML

TOTAL TIME: 15 MINUTES

245ml double cream

1 teaspoon vanilla extract

220g caster sugar

1 heaped teaspoon sea salt

Gently warm the cream and vanilla extract in a small pan over a low heat. Meanwhile, place the sugar and 6 tablespoons of water in a separate pan over a high heat and bring to the boil, making sure not to stir the mixture at all. Allow to boil and bubble for 5 to 8 minutes, or until it turns a deep, bright amber colour. Keep an eye on it – as soon as it's ready, remove from the heat, then gradually add the warm vanilla cream, stirring continuously (the mixture may hiss and bubble at first, so take extra care because it'll be extremely hot). If lumps start to form, speed up your stirring, and if any remain at the end, reheat the mixture on a very low heat, stirring continuously to get rid of them.

As the caramel starts to cool, sprinkle in the salt (I like the coarse, flaked kind) and pour the mixture into an airtight container. Use straight away or store in the fridge for up to 2 weeks (unless someone scoffs the lot with a brownie and some vanilla ice cream).

Do you need to take a cupcake from uh-huh to woo-hoo in 10 seconds flat? This addictively sweet and salty sauce pops up a lot in these recipes, and there's very little in the cake world (possibly even in the whole world) that wouldn't benefit from a little drop of this magic stuff.

Brittle

TOTAL TIME: 15 MINUTES
PLUS COOLING

vegetable oil, for greasing

2 tablespoons black and white
sesame seeds or 40g pecan nuts
(see tip below)

220g caster sugar

1 tablespoon unsalted butter

YOU NEED

optional: sugar thermometer

Before you start, lightly oil a spatula and a 25cm x 35cm baking tray. Roughly chop the pecans (if using) and put to one side. Warm the sugar and 4 tablespoons of water in a pan over a low heat for a few minutes, or until the sugar dissolves, swirling the pan occasionally. Turn the heat up to medium and allow to bubble and boil for a further 5 minutes, or until it turns a light amber colour, making sure not to stir the mixture at all. Keep an eye on it – if it starts to crystallize, don't worry, just keep going. As soon as it's ready, remove from the heat (if you have a sugar thermometer this is at around 165°C).

Working quickly, add the butter, stirring continuously with the oiled spatula until any frothing has subsided and the mixture is velvety smooth. Stir in the seeds or chopped nuts, then very carefully pour the mixture on to the oiled baking tray, smoothing it out evenly – the caramel is basically hotter than the surface of the sun at this point, so be very careful. Leave aside to cool completely and harden, then break the brittle into pieces. Use straight away or store in a dry, airtight container. It'll keep for around 2 weeks at room temperature, but if you're anything like us, it won't last that long!

These brittle pieces are perfect for my **banana, maple & pecan cupcakes** (see page 118) and **green tea cupcakes** (see page 46), but you can always experiment with different combinations of nuts and seeds to see what you come up with. You could even add some fresh citrus zest or chilli for an extra kick.

Infused milk

MAKES
200ML

200ml whole milk

2 heaped tablespoons of your
chosen flavouring, such as lightly
bashed cardamom pods, Earl Grey
tea leaves, Chai tea leaves, dried
lavender flowers, fresh mint leaves

Infusing milk with natural aromatics is a great way of getting amazing flavours into your cupcakes. Simply place the milk and your chosen flavouring in a small pan over a medium heat. Bring the milk almost to the boil – keep a close eye on it – then reduce the heat to low and simmer gently for around 2 minutes. Remove the pan from the heat, cover with a lid and leave to cool completely. Once cooled, strain through a sieve and use straight away, or store in an airtight container in the fridge.

Try experimenting with different herbs, teas and dried flowers. Rooibos, lapsang souchong or other loose-leaf teas all work well, as will fresh herbs such as rosemary, basil and thyme. Fruits, and even fruit teas, are best avoided because they can curdle the milk.

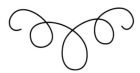

Fruit goo

MAKES 250ML

TOTAL TIME: 20 MINUTES

400g fresh or frozen fruit, such as raspberries, strawberries, blueberries, cherries (see tip below)

110g caster sugar

optional: 1 lemon

Using fresh fruit sauces, or 'goos', as we lovingly call them at Crumbs & Doilies HQ, is a great way to add brilliant natural flavour and excitement to your cupcakes. They can be drizzled over the top, folded into icings or sponges, or even piped into the middle of cupcakes for a hidden jammy treat.

Place your chosen fruit and the sugar in a pan over a medium heat and bring to a gentle simmer. Reduce the heat and allow the mixture to bubble gently for 10 to 15 minutes, or until thickened, stirring occasionally. Firmer fruit, such as blueberries, will take longer to break down, so you can help them along by crushing them slightly with a potato masher or the back of a spoon.

Once thick, remove from the heat and strain the fruit goo through a sieve while it's still warm, using the back of a spoon to push as much of the liquid through as you can. Have a taste and add some more sugar or fresh lemon juice (if needed), until you've got just the right sweetness, then pour into an airtight container and leave to cool. Use straight away, store in the fridge for up to 2 weeks, or freeze and use it whenever you fancy. I love using leftovers on ice cream or stirred through my morning porridge.

Blueberries, cherries and other firm fruits such as apricots tend to release a lot of liquid, rather than a nice, thick fruity goo. Solve this by adding 2 to 3 tablespoons of agar flakes to the mixture before it goes on the heat, or simply simmer for longer to reduce.

Spring

New starts, fresh air, prancing about, blossom-heavy breezes and the promise of sunshine – cakes to make you smile.

Earl Grey breakfast cupcakes

TOTAL TIME: 1 HOUR 15 MINUTES
PLUS COOLING

FOR THE CUPCAKES

3 slices of brown bread

250g unsalted butter, plus extra
for spreading, softened

250g self-raising flour

250g caster sugar

½ teaspoon bicarbonate of soda

4 large free-range eggs

3 tablespoons Earl Grey **infused
milk** (see page 32)

½ x 450g jar of fine-cut marmalade

FOR THE BUTTERCREAM ICING

300g unsalted butter, softened

675g icing sugar

6 tablespoons Earl Grey **infused
milk** (see page 32)

YOU NEED

2 x 12-hole muffin trays,
with snug-fitting paper cases

1 x piping bag (with 5mm nozzle)

Preheat the oven to 170°C fan/375°F/gas 5. Toast the bread until slightly burnt, then butter both sides and bake in the oven for 5 to 10 minutes, or until crisp enough to snap. Remove and leave to cool, then whiz in a food processor or grate with a box grater and set aside. Sift the remaining dry cupcake ingredients into a large bowl, add the butter and eggs, then beat for 60 seconds with an electric mixer (I prefer the free-standing type). Add the Earl Grey **infused milk** and whisk for 20 seconds, or until well combined. Scrape down the sides of the bowl with a spatula, then give the mix a final blast for 30 seconds to make sure it's all incorporated. Fill the paper cases two-thirds full with mixture, but don't bother to smooth it out. Bake for 20 minutes, or until they spring back when touched. Leave to cool, transferring to a wire cooling rack after 5 minutes.

Meanwhile, make the icing. Beat the butter with an electric mixer for 4 to 5 minutes, or until pale and smooth. Sift the icing sugar into a large bowl, then add to the butter in two stages, beating well between each. Gradually add the Earl Grey **infused milk** and beat for a further 3 to 5 minutes, or until well combined. Once the cupcakes are cool, poke a hole into the middle of each with a chopstick, twist to widen the hole, then use a piping bag to fill each one with a little marmalade. Decorate with the icing, sprinkle over the buttered toast crumbs and serve.

This cupcake reminds me of my grandma Mabel's quintessentially English breakfasts in Wallasey (minus the Cheshire cheese, which I always thought was a little odd).

Pistachio & rose cupcakes

**TOTAL TIME: 45 MINUTES
PLUS COOLING**

FOR THE CUPCAKES

75g shelled unsalted pistachios

250g self-raising flour

250g caster sugar

½ teaspoon bicarbonate of soda

250g unsalted butter, softened

4 large free-range eggs

½ teaspoon vanilla extract

1 teaspoon rose water

3 tablespoons whole milk

optional: crystallized
rose petals (see tip below)

FOR THE BUTTERCREAM ICING

300g unsalted butter, softened

¼ teaspoon vanilla extract

½ teaspoon rose water

optional: pink food-colouring paste

4 tablespoons whole milk

675g icing sugar

YOU NEED

2 x 12-hole muffin trays,
with snug-fitting paper cases

Preheat the oven to 170°C fan/375°F/gas 5. Roughly chop the pistachios and put into a large bowl, then sift in the remaining dry cupcake ingredients (apart from the rose petals). Add the butter and eggs and beat for 60 seconds with an electric mixer (I prefer the free-standing type). Stir the vanilla extract and rose water into the milk, then add to the mix and whisk for 20 seconds, or until well combined. Scrape down the sides of the bowl with a spatula, then give the mix a final blast for 30 seconds to make sure it's all incorporated. Fill the paper cases two-thirds full with mixture, but don't bother to smooth it out. Bake for 20 minutes, or until they spring back when touched. Leave to cool, transferring to a wire cooling rack after 5 minutes.

Meanwhile, make the icing. Beat the butter with an electric mixer for 4 to 5 minutes, or until pale and smooth. Stir the vanilla extract, rose water and food colouring (if using) into the milk and set aside. Sift the icing sugar into a large bowl, then add to the butter in two stages, beating well between each. Gradually add the vanilla milk and beat for a further 3 to 5 minutes, or until smooth. Once the cupcakes are cool, decorate them with the icing – if you've got a rose or star-shaped nozzle and a piping bag, use them here to make the cakes look extra rosy. Top with some crystallized rose petals for an extra touch of class.

If you can't find crystallized rose petals, make them yourself: brush some fresh rose petals with whisked, frothy egg white, then coat in caster sugar and leave to dry overnight.

Raspberry ripple layer cake

TOTAL TIME: 1 HOUR 30 MINUTES
PLUS COOLING

FOR THE SPONGE

375g unsalted butter, plus extra
for greasing, softened

375g caster sugar

6 large free-range eggs

375g self-raising flour

¾ teaspoon vanilla extract

4½ tablespoons whole milk

1 x raspberry **fruit goo**
(see page 34)

350g fresh raspberries

FOR THE BUTTERCREAM ICING

1 x **vanilla buttercream icing**
(see page 16)

YOU NEED

3 x 20cm sandwich cake tins,
greased and lined

Preheat the oven to 170°C fan/375°F/gas 5. Place the butter and sugar in a large bowl, then beat with an electric mixer (I prefer the free-standing type) for 5 to 7 minutes, or until light and fluffy. Crack in the eggs one at a time, whisking well before adding the next – if the mixture starts to split, whisk in 1 tablespoon of the flour. Stir the vanilla extract into the milk and set aside. Sift the flour into the mixture and fold through, but don't mix too much at this stage. Pour in the vanilla milk and mix gently to combine.

Equally divide the mixture between the prepared cake tins, smoothing it out with a spatula. Evenly distribute half the raspberry **fruit goo** between the tins, swirling it through the mixture to create a rippled effect. Bake the cakes for 25 minutes, or until an inserted skewer comes out clean, then turn them out on to a wire cooling rack and leave to cool.

Once the cakes have cooled, use a sharp serrated knife to trim the tops off them to make the surfaces nice and flat, then carefully halve each sponge horizontally so you end up with six rounds. Spread a quarter of the **vanilla buttercream icing** onto a round and tear over a handful of raspberries. Place another sponge on top and spread with a thin layer of raspberry fruit goo. Repeat with the other sponges, topping them with alternate layers of icing and raspberries, and fruit goo, then finish with the remaining sponge. Use a palette knife to smooth the sides and the top of the cake with the remaining icing, then top with raspberries and serve.

This cake is the jammiest, fluffiest, yummiest cake we've ever made at Crumbs & Doilies. If raspberries aren't in season, you can use frozen ones instead, just make sure you defrost them first.

Chocolate Guinness cupcakes

MAKES
24

TOTAL TIME: 50 MINUTES
PLUS COOLING

FOR THE CUPCAKES

250ml Guinness original stout

250g unsalted butter, cubed

75g cocoa powder

400g caster sugar

2 large free-range eggs

1 teaspoon vanilla extract

140ml soured cream

225g plain flour

2½ teaspoons bicarbonate of soda

FOR THE CREAM CHEESE ICING

1 x **cream cheese icing**
(see page 20)

YOU NEED

2 x 12-hole muffin trays,
with snug-fitting paper cases

Preheat the oven to 160°C fan/350°F/gas 4. Place the Guinness and butter in a pan over a medium heat and allow the butter to melt, but make sure it doesn't boil. Whisk in the cocoa powder and sugar until dissolved, then remove from the heat and allow to cool slightly.

Crack the eggs into a large bowl, add the vanilla extract and soured cream, then beat until well combined with an electric mixer (I prefer the free-standing type). Gradually pour in the Guinness mixture, whisking continuously. Mix the flour and bicarbonate of soda together in a bowl, then add to the wet mixture, beating continuously until silky smooth. Transfer the mixture to a small jug (you'll need to do this in batches), and carefully fill the paper cases just over two-thirds full. Bake for 20 minutes, or until they spring back when touched. Leave to cool, transferring to a wire cooling rack after 5 minutes, then decorate with **cream cheese icing** and a few sprinkles and enjoy.

My mum always swore she drank half a pint of Guinness a week when she was pregnant with me (something about Guinness being 'good' for you . . .). Anyway, even if Guinness isn't your go-to beverage, don't be put off here – I know plenty of people who flat-out hate it, but have been totally seduced by these guys.

Green tea cupcakes with sesame brittle

MAKES
24

FOR THE CUPCAKES

250g self-raising flour

½ teaspoon bicarbonate of soda

250g caster sugar

1 heaped teaspoon matcha
green tea powder

270g unsalted butter, softened

4 large free-range eggs

¼ teaspoon vanilla extract

3 tablespoons whole milk

FOR THE BUTTERCREAM ICING

300g unsalted butter, softened

¼ teaspoon vanilla extract

4 tablespoons whole milk

660g icing sugar

1 tablespoon matcha
green tea powder

FOR THE BRITTLE

1 x black and white sesame **brittle**
(see page 30)

YOU NEED

2 x 12-hole muffin trays,
with snug-fitting paper cases

Preheat the oven to 170°C fan/375°F/gas 5. Sift the dry cupcake ingredients into a large bowl, add the butter and eggs, then beat for 60 seconds with an electric mixer (I prefer the free-standing type). Stir the vanilla extract into the milk, then add to the mix and whisk for another 20 seconds, or until well combined. Scrape down the sides of the bowl with a spatula, then give the mix a final blast for 30 seconds to make sure it's all incorporated. Fill the paper cases two-thirds full with mixture, but don't bother to smooth it out. Bake for 20 minutes, or until they spring back when touched. Leave to cool, transferring to a wire cooling rack after 5 minutes.

Meanwhile, make the icing. Beat the butter with an electric mixer for 4 to 5 minutes, or until pale and smooth. Stir the vanilla extract into the milk and set aside. Sift the icing sugar into a large bowl with the green tea powder, then add to the butter in two stages, beating well between each. Gradually add the vanilla milk and beat for a further 3 to 5 minutes, or until well combined. Once the cupcakes are cool, decorate them with the icing, top with shards of sesame **brittle** and tuck in.

These cupcakes are subtly flavoured with green tea, but there's nothing subtle about their appearance – they are green, people! With shards of black and white sesame brittle poking out of the top, these cupcakes make really exciting dinner treats.

Lemon & poppy seed cupcakes

MAKES 24

TOTAL TIME: 45 MINUTES
PLUS COOLING

FOR THE CUPCAKES

250g self-raising flour

250g caster sugar

½ teaspoon bicarbonate of soda

1½ tablespoons poppy seeds, plus extra for decorating

250g unsalted butter, softened

4 large free-range eggs

1½ tablespoons lemon juice

optional: zest from 4 unwaxed lemons

1½ tablespoons whole milk

FOR THE CREAM CHEESE ICING

1 x **cream cheese icing** (see page 20)

YOU NEED

2 x 12-hole muffin trays, with snug-fitting paper cases

Preheat the oven to 170°C fan/375°F/gas 5. Sift the dry cupcake ingredients into a large bowl. Add the butter, eggs, lemon juice and most of the zest (if using), then beat for 60 seconds with an electric mixer (I prefer the free-standing type). Add the milk and beat for another 20 seconds, or until well combined. Scrape down the sides of the bowl with a spatula, then give the mix a final blast for 30 seconds to make sure it's all incorporated. Fill the paper cases two-thirds full with mixture, but don't bother to smooth it out. Bake for 20 minutes, or until they spring back when touched.

Leave to cool, transferring to a wire cooling rack after 5 minutes, then decorate with the **cream cheese icing**, sprinkle with poppy seeds and the remaining lemon zest, then serve.

They may be tiny, but poppy seeds are packed with a subtle, nutty, peppery flavour that goes perfectly with the zesty lemon sponge.

Cookie dough cupcakes

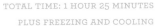

TOTAL TIME: 1 HOUR 25 MINUTES
PLUS FREEZING AND COOLING

FOR THE CUPCAKES

260g unsalted butter, cubed

130g caster sugar

120g soft dark brown sugar

40g dark chocolate (70%)

250g self-raising flour

½ teaspoon bicarbonate of soda

4 large free-range eggs

3 tablespoons whole milk

FOR THE COOKIE DOUGH

50g dark chocolate (70%)

160g plain flour

130g caster sugar

4 tablespoons demerara sugar

170g unsalted butter, softened

2 tablespoons soya yoghurt

2 teaspoons vanilla extract

FOR THE BUTTERCREAM ICING

1 x **vanilla buttercream icing**
(see page 16)

YOU NEED

2 x 12-hole muffin trays,
with snug-fitting paper cases

Preheat the oven to 170°C fan/375°F/gas 5. For the cookie dough, finely chop the chocolate (this is best done in a food processor), then tip into a large bowl. Whisk in the remaining cookie dough ingredients and 1 teaspoon of fine sea salt with an electric mixer (I prefer the free-standing type), and beat to a sticky dough. Place on a piece of clingfilm and flatten to roughly 1.5cm thick, then wrap up and place in the freezer for around 2 hours to firm up.

Now for the cupcakes! Place 200g of butter in a pan over a medium heat and cook for 5 to 6 minutes, or until rich and golden in colour, stirring continuously. Transfer to a heatproof bowl and leave to cool, then place in the fridge for 15 to 20 minutes, or until set to a spreadable consistency, stirring occasionally. Meanwhile, whisk the sugars with an electric mixer to get rid of any lumps, then finely chop the chocolate and add to the bowl. Sift in the remaining dry cupcake ingredients and 1 pinch of salt. Add the burnt butter, eggs and the remaining 60g of butter (softened), then beat for 60 seconds. Add the milk and beat for another 20 seconds, or until well combined. Scrape down the sides of the bowl with a spatula, then give the mix a final blast for 30 seconds to make sure it's all incorporated.

Fill the paper cases two-thirds full with the cake mixture, but don't bother to smooth it out. Chop the frozen cookie dough into chunks (about 1.5cm thick) and divide half of them between the cases. Bake for 20 minutes, or until they spring back when touched. Leave to cool, transferring to a wire cooling rack after 5 minutes. Decorate them with the **vanilla buttercream icing**, top each with a lump of the frozen cookie dough and enjoy.

> Cookie dough is almost as delicious raw as it is cooked, so here's a recipe which gives it the respect it deserves, with no raw egg to worry about.

Pistachio, lime & cardamom cake

SERVES
10

TOTAL TIME: 1 HOUR 20 MINUTES
PLUS COOLING

FOR THE SPONGE

185g caster sugar

½ teaspoon baking powder

185g self-raising flour

½ teaspoon ground cardamom

150g shelled unsalted pistachios,
plus extra for decorating

150g unsalted butter, plus extra
for greasing, softened

3 large free-range eggs

125g plain yoghurt

FOR THE LIME SYRUP

125g caster sugar

zest from 1 unwaxed lime
and juice from 2

YOU NEED

1 x 20cm springform cake tin,
greased and lined

Preheat the oven to 170°C fan/375°F/gas 5. Place the sugar, baking powder, flour and cardamom in a large bowl. Finely chop and add the pistachios, along with the butter and eggs, then beat for 60 seconds with an electric mixer (I prefer the free-standing type). Add the yoghurt and whisk well to combine. Scrape down the sides of the bowl with a spatula and give the mix a final blast for 30 seconds to make sure it's all incorporated. Pour it into the prepared tin, smoothing it out with a spatula. Bake for around 1 hour on the middle shelf of the oven, or until an inserted skewer comes out clean, then leave to cool slightly in the tin.

Meanwhile, make the lime syrup. Place the sugar, lime juice and 75ml of water in a small pan over a low heat. Cook gently for 3 to 4 minutes, or until the sugar has dissolved, stirring continuously. Turn the heat up to medium and bring to the boil, then add the lime zest and cook for a further 5 minutes, or until syrupy and reduced. Sieve the syrup into a bowl and leave to cool slightly. Turn the warm cake out on to a wire cooling rack and use a cocktail stick to poke small holes all over the top, then pour over the lime syrup. Finely chop and sprinkle over some more pistachios to decorate, then leave to cool completely before serving.

This was one of the first cakes I made for my very first market stall on Brick Lane. The citrusy and fragrant flavour of the cardamom adds a touch of the exotic to this light, moist and totally addictive cake.

Hot cross bun cupcakes

MAKES
24

TOTAL TIME: 45 MINUTES
PLUS SOAKING AND COOLING

FOR THE CUPCAKES

25g currants

100ml fresh unsweetened
orange juice

250g self-raising flour

¼ teaspoon bicarbonate of soda

200g caster sugar

50g soft dark brown sugar

¼ teaspoon ground cinnamon

¾ teaspoon mixed spice

40g mixed peel

270g unsalted butter, softened

4 large free-range eggs

3 tablespoons whole milk

½ tablespoon golden syrup

4 heaped tablespoons apricot jam

FOR THE BUTTERCREAM ICING

½ x **vanilla buttercream icing**
(see page 16)

optional: Angostura bitters

YOU NEED

2 x 12-hole muffin trays,
with snug-fitting paper cases

1 x piping bag (with 5mm nozzle)

Preheat the oven to 170°C fan/375°F/gas 5. Before you start, soak the currants in the orange juice for around 30 minutes, then drain. Put the dry cupcake ingredients and the soaked currants into a large bowl, then stir to combine. Add the butter and eggs, then beat for 60 seconds with an electric mixer (I prefer the free-standing type). Add the milk and golden syrup, then whisk for 20 seconds, or until well combined. Scrape down the sides of the bowl with a spatula, then give the mix a final blast for 30 seconds to make sure it's all incorporated. Fill the paper cases two-thirds full with mixture, but don't bother to smooth it out. Bake for 20 minutes, or until they spring back when touched, then leave to cool slightly in the trays.

Meanwhile, warm the apricot jam over a medium heat and brush over the warm cupcakes, then place them on a wire cooling rack to cool completely. In the meantime, make the **vanilla buttercream icing**, mixing in 2–3 dashes of Angostura bitters (if you have some to hand), to taste. Once the cupcakes are cool, pipe a cross of icing onto each of them and serve.

I love Easter, mainly because for three or four solid weeks you are never more than a few feet away from a hot cross bun. Here we have all the flavours of a hot cross bun, magically transformed into a cupcake.

Vegan vanilla fudge cupcakes

TOTAL TIME: 45 MINUTES
PLUS COOLING

FOR THE CUPCAKES

300g caster sugar

150ml sunflower oil

1 teaspoon vanilla extract

500g dairy-free soya yoghurt

2 teaspoons cider vinegar

360g plain flour

1 teaspoon bicarbonate of soda

1½ teaspoons baking powder

FOR THE VEGAN VANILLA ICING

200g dairy-free soya spread, chilled

660g icing sugar

½ teaspoon vanilla extract

YOU NEED

2 x 12-hole muffin trays,
with snug-fitting paper cases

Preheat the oven to 170°C fan/375°F/gas 5. Place the sugar, oil and vanilla extract in a large bowl, then beat with an electric mixer (I prefer the free-standing type) for 1 to 2 minutes, until well combined. Mix the yoghurt and vinegar together in a bowl, then add to the mixture and beat for 1 to 2 minutes. Add the remaining cupcake ingredients and 1 teaspoon of fine sea salt, then whisk until smooth and just combined. Fill the paper cases two-thirds full with mixture, but don't bother to smooth it out. Bake for 20 minutes, or until they spring back when touched. Leave to cool, transferring to a wire cooling rack after 5 minutes.

Meanwhile, make the icing. Beat the soya spread with an electric mixer for 1 to 2 minutes, or until smooth. Sift the icing sugar into a large bowl, then add to the soya spread in two stages, beating well between each. Add the vanilla extract and a small splash of water, then whisk for a further few minutes, or until silky smooth – if it's too stiff, add a splash more water to loosen. Once the cupcakes are cool, decorate them with the icing and add a few sprinkles too if you like – whatever takes your fancy – then enjoy.

> These are irresistible for vegans and non-vegans alike.
> If you want to make them non-vegan, feel free to use
> **vanilla buttercream icing** (see page 16) instead.

Summer

Days in the park, drives in the country and good times in the sunshine – cakes that are fruity, floral and fun.

Lemon mess cupcakes

 MAKES 24

TOTAL TIME: 1 HOUR 35 MINUTES
PLUS COOLING

FOR THE CUPCAKES

250g self-raising flour

250g caster sugar

½ teaspoon bicarbonate of soda

270g unsalted butter, softened

4 large free-range eggs

zest from 4 unwaxed lemons
and 1½ tablespoons lemon juice

1½ tablespoons whole milk

½ x 325g jar of quality lemon curd

FOR THE BUTTERCREAM ICING

300g unsalted butter, softened

675g icing sugar

4 tablespoons lemon juice

5 **meringues** (see page 24)

YOU NEED

2 x 12-hole muffin trays,
with snug-fitting paper cases

1 x piping bag (with 5mm nozzle)

Preheat the oven to 170°C fan/375°F/gas 5. Sift the dry cupcake ingredients into a large bowl, add the butter, eggs, lemon zest and juice, then beat for 60 seconds with an electric mixer (I prefer the free-standing type). Pour in the milk and beat for another 20 seconds, or until well combined. Scrape down the sides of the bowl with a spatula, then give the mix a final blast for 30 seconds to make sure it's all incorporated. Fill the paper cases two-thirds full with mixture, but don't bother to smooth it out. Bake for 20 minutes, or until they spring back when touched. Leave to cool, transferring to a wire cooling rack after 5 minutes.

Meanwhile, make the icing. Beat the butter with an electric mixer for 4 to 5 minutes, or until pale and smooth. Sift the icing sugar into a large bowl, then add to the butter in two stages, beating well between each. Gradually add the lemon juice and beat for a further 3 to 5 minutes, or until well combined. Break the **meringues** into small pieces and fold through the icing. Once the cupcakes are cool, poke a hole into the middle of each with a chopstick, twist to widen the hole, then use a piping bag to fill each one with a little lemon curd. Top each with a dollop of icing (be as messy as you like!), drizzle over the remaining lemon curd and enjoy.

Use shop-bought meringues if you like, but I always like to make my own. For added oomph, serve with a sprinkling of pie crumble on top – see my **cherry Bakewell cupcakes** (page 74) for how to make it.

Blueberry cheesecake cupcakes

MAKES 24

TOTAL TIME: 1 HOUR 10 MINUTES
PLUS COOLING

FOR THE CUPCAKES

250g self-raising flour

250g caster sugar

½ teaspoon bicarbonate of soda

270g unsalted butter, softened

4 large free-range eggs

zest from 1 unwaxed lemon
and 1½ tablespoons lemon juice

1½ tablespoons whole milk

1 x blueberry **fruit goo**
(see page 34)

FOR THE BUTTERY BISCUIT BASE

50g unsalted butter, cubed

175g digestive biscuits

1 tablespoon golden syrup

FOR THE MASCARPONE ICING

150g unsalted butter, softened

240g mascarpone

840g icing sugar

YOU NEED

2 x 12-hole muffin trays,
with snug-fitting paper cases

1 x piping bag (with 5mm nozzle)

Preheat the oven to 170°C fan/375°F/gas 5. For the buttery biscuit base, melt the butter in a small pan over a low heat, then blitz the biscuits to fine crumbs in a food processor. Combine both with the golden syrup, then scoop 1 tablespoon of the mixture into each paper case, pressing down to make a nice firm base. Sift the dry cupcake ingredients into a large bowl, add the butter, eggs, lemon zest and juice, then beat for 60 seconds with an electric mixer (I prefer the free-standing type). Add the milk and beat for another 20 seconds, or until well combined. Scrape down the sides of the bowl with a spatula, then give the mix a final blast for 30 seconds to make sure it's all incorporated. Fill the paper cases two-thirds full with mixture, but don't bother to smooth it out. Bake for 20 minutes, or until they spring back when touched. Leave to cool, transferring to a wire cooling rack after 5 minutes.

Meanwhile, make the icing. Beat the butter and mascarpone with an electric mixer for 2 to 3 minutes, or until pale and smooth. Sift the icing sugar into a large bowl, then add to the butter in two stages, beating well between each – if the mix seems too loose, add a little more icing sugar until the consistency is just right. Once the cupcakes are cool, poke a hole into the middle of each with a chopstick, twist to widen the hole, then use a piping bag to fill each one with a good squeeze of the blueberry **fruit goo**. Decorate with the icing, add a few small blobs of fruit goo to each one and swirl them through the icing with a cocktail stick, and enjoy.

> Whenever we make these cupcakes at Crumbs & Doilies, we sing along to Cassetteboy's Greg Wallace buttery biscuit base song on YouTube – look it up!

Rosemary, honey & yoghurt loaf

SERVES 12

FOR THE LOAF

160ml olive oil, plus
extra for greasing

365ml plain yoghurt

3 large free-range eggs

½ teaspoon vanilla extract

1 sprig of fresh rosemary,
leaves picked

310g self-raising flour

285g caster sugar

½ teaspoon bicarbonate of soda

1 pinch of ground nutmeg

FOR THE YOGHURT ICING

375g icing sugar

150g plain yoghurt

75ml runny honey

YOU NEED

1 x 1.5 litre loaf tin,
greased and lined

Preheat the oven to 170°C fan/375°F/gas 5. Place the oil, yoghurt, eggs and vanilla extract in a large bowl, then beat until well combined with an electric mixer (I prefer the free-standing type). Finely chop and add the rosemary leaves, along with all the remaining loaf ingredients and ¼ of a teaspoon of fine sea salt, then beat on a low speed for around 2 minutes, or until silky smooth. Fill the prepared loaf tin with the mixture and smooth it out with a spatula. Bake for 45 minutes, or until an inserted skewer comes out clean, then leave to cool slightly in the tin.

Meanwhile, sift the icing sugar into a large bowl, then add the yoghurt and 1 tablespoon of honey and beat with an electric mixer for a further 2 minutes, or until it resembles the consistency of double cream – add a bit more honey if it's too stiff or a little more icing sugar if it's too runny, until you get it just right.

By now, your kitchen should be filled with a wonderful cakey smell, reminiscent of a sun-drenched Grecian hillside – or something like that. Turn the still-warm cake out on to a wire cooling rack and use a cocktail stick to poke small holes all over the top, then drizzle over the remaining honey – if you want more of a drizzling consistency, gently warm the honey first. Leave the cake to cool while the honey soaks in, then once cool, decorate with the icing and a drizzle more honey if you like, then serve immediately.

> I've found the thought of adding rosemary to cakes sometimes puts people off, but when combined with the Mediterranean flavours of honey and yoghurt, this teatime treat is certain to convert the non-believers.

Eton mess cupcakes

MAKES 24

FOR THE CUPCAKES

250g self-raising flour

½ teaspoon bicarbonate of soda

250g caster sugar

250g unsalted butter, softened

4 large free-range eggs

7–8 tablespoons strawberry or raspberry **fruit goo** (see page 34)

FOR THE BUTTERCREAM ICING

5 **meringues** (see page 24)

1 x **vanilla buttercream icing** (see page 16)

YOU NEED

2 x 12-hole muffin trays, with snug-fitting paper cases

Preheat the oven to 170°C fan/375°F/gas 5. Sift the dry cupcake ingredients into a large bowl, add the butter and eggs, then beat for 60 seconds with an electric mixer (I prefer the free-standing type). Add 3 tablespoons of **fruit goo** and beat for 20 seconds, or until well combined. Scrape down the sides of the bowl with a spatula, then give the mix a final blast for 30 seconds to make sure it's all incorporated. Fill the paper cases two-thirds full with mixture, but don't bother to smooth it out. Bake for 20 minutes, or until they spring back when touched. Leave to cool, transferring to a wire cooling rack after 5 minutes.

Meanwhile, make the icing. Crush the **meringues** into small pieces and fold through the **vanilla buttercream icing**. Once the cupcakes are cool, top each one with a dollop of the icing – it's called Eton mess for a reason, so don't worry about being too neat here; think rustic charm, rather than perfect patisserie. Drizzle over the remaining **fruit goo** and tuck in.

It's much more satisfying to make your own meringues, but feel free to use shop-bought ones if you want to.

Mojito cupcakes

MAKES 24

TOTAL TIME: 50 MINUTES
PLUS COOLING

FOR THE CUPCAKES

250g self-raising flour

250g caster sugar

½ teaspoon bicarbonate of soda

zest from 3 unwaxed limes
and 1½ tablespoons lime juice

275g unsalted butter, softened

4 large free-range eggs

1½ tablespoons mint **infused milk**
(see page 32)

24 crystallized mint leaves
(see tip below)

FOR THE BUTTERCREAM ICING

300g unsalted butter, softened

675g icing sugar

3 tablespoons dark rum

2 tablespoons mint **infused milk**
(see page 32)

YOU NEED

2 x 12-hole muffin trays,
with snug-fitting paper cases

Preheat the oven to 170°C fan/375°F/gas 5. Sift the dry cupcake ingredients into a large bowl (apart from the mint leaves), add the lime zest and juice, butter and eggs, then beat for 60 seconds with an electric mixer (I prefer the free-standing type). Add the mint **infused milk** and beat for 20 seconds, or until well combined. Scrape down the sides of the bowl with a spatula, then give the mix a final blast for 30 seconds to make sure it's all incorporated. Fill the paper cases two-thirds full with mixture, but don't bother to smooth it out. Bake for 20 minutes, or until they spring back when touched. Leave to cool, transferring to a wire cooling rack after 5 minutes.

Meanwhile, make the icing. Beat the butter with an electric mixer for 4 to 5 minutes, or until pale and smooth. Sift the icing sugar into a large bowl, then add to the butter in two stages, beating well between each. Gradually add the rum and the mint **infused milk** and beat for a further 3 to 5 minutes, or until well combined. Once the cupcakes are cool, decorate them with the icing and top each with a crystallized mint leaf – these taste like summer holidays!

> If you can't find crystallized mint leaves, make them yourself. Brush some fresh mint leaves with whisked, frothy egg white, then coat in caster sugar and leave to dry overnight.

Super-lemony meringue cake

SERVES 16

TOTAL TIME: 1 HOUR 15 MINUTES
PLUS COOLING

FOR THE SPONGE

375g unsalted butter, plus extra
for greasing, softened

375g caster sugar

6 large free-range eggs

375g self-raising flour

zest from 6 unwaxed lemons
and 1½ tablespoons lemon juice

2 tablespoons whole milk

FOR THE FILLINGS

200g unsalted butter, softened

450g icing sugar

3 tablespoons lemon juice

¾ x 325g jar of quality lemon curd

FOR THE MERINGUE ICING

1 x **marshmallowy meringue icing**
(see page 26)

YOU NEED

3 x 20cm sandwich cake tins,
greased and lined

optional: 1 x blowtorch

Preheat the oven to 170°C fan/375°F/gas 5. For the sponge, place the butter and sugar in a large bowl, then beat with an electric mixer (I prefer the free-standing type) for 5 to 7 minutes, or until light and fluffy. Crack in the eggs one at a time, whisking well before adding the next – if the mixture starts to split, whisk in 1 tablespoon of the flour. Add the lemon zest and sift in the flour, then fold through. Pour in the lemon juice and milk and mix to combine.

Equally divide the mixture between the prepared cake tins, smoothing it out with a spatula. Bake the cakes for 25 minutes, or until an inserted skewer comes out clean, then turn them out on to a wire cooling rack and leave to cool.

Meanwhile, make the buttercream filling. Beat the butter with an electric mixer for 4 to 5 minutes, or until pale and smooth. Sift the icing sugar into a large bowl, then add to the butter in two stages, beating well between each. Add the lemon juice and beat for a further 3 to 5 minutes, or until almost white.

Once the cakes have cooled, use a sharp serrated knife to trim the tops off them to make the surfaces nice and flat, then carefully halve each sponge horizontally so you end up with six rounds. Spread one-fifth of the lemon curd on to a round, then spread over one-fifth of the buttercream filling. Layer over another sponge, top with another layer of lemon curd and buttercream, and repeat three more times. Finish with the remaining sponge and use a palette knife to smooth the sides and the top of the cake with the **marshmallowy meringue icing**, then serve.

> If you want to take this to another level, blast the topping with a blowtorch. It's still pretty good without the toasting, but blowtorching stuff is fun – just be very careful!

Lavender caramel cupcakes

MAKES 24

TOTAL TIME: 50 MINUTES
PLUS COOLING

FOR THE CUPCAKES

250g self-raising flour

250g caster sugar

½ teaspoon bicarbonate of soda

250g unsalted butter, softened

4 large free-range eggs

3 tablespoons lavender
infused milk (see page 32)

FOR THE LAVENDER CARAMEL

1 heaped tablespoon dried
lavender flowers

245ml double cream

220g caster sugar

FOR THE BUTTERCREAM ICING

300g unsalted butter, softened

530g icing sugar

YOU NEED

2 x 12-hole muffin trays,
with snug-fitting paper cases

Preheat the oven to 170°C fan/375°F/gas 5. Put 110ml boiling water and the lavender flowers into a bowl, then set aside to infuse until needed. Sift the dry cupcake ingredients into a large bowl, add the butter and eggs, then beat for 60 seconds with an electric mixer (I prefer the free-standing type). Add the lavender **infused milk** and beat for 20 seconds, or until well combined. Scrape down the sides of the bowl with a spatula, then give the mix a final blast for 30 seconds to make sure it's all incorporated. Fill the paper cases two-thirds full with mixture, but don't bother to smooth it out. Bake for 20 minutes, or until they spring back when touched. Leave to cool, transferring to a wire cooling rack after 5 minutes.

For the lavender caramel, use the ingredients here to follow the **salted caramel** method (see page 28 – you don't need the vanilla extract or salt). Replace the water with all of your lavender infused water, making sure you strain it first. It'll froth up a lot more than regular caramel, so you'll need to use your instincts to work out when the sugar has caramelized – there should be a hint of almost burnt sugar and a strong smell of lavender.

For the icing, beat the butter with an electric mixer for 4 to 5 minutes, or until pale and smooth. Sift the icing sugar into a large bowl, then add to the butter in two stages, beating well between each. Add just over half of the lavender caramel and beat for a further 3 to 5 minutes, or until silky smooth. Once the cupcakes are cool, decorate them with the icing, drizzle over the remaining lavender caramel and enjoy.

Cherry Bakewell cupcakes

MAKES
24

TOTAL TIME: 1 HOUR
PLUS COOLING

FOR THE CUPCAKES

70g ground almonds

180g self-raising flour

250g caster sugar

½ teaspoon bicarbonate of soda

250g unsalted butter, softened

4 large free-range eggs

¼ teaspoon almond extract

3 tablespoons whole milk

50g flaked almonds

FOR THE PIE CRUMBLE TOPPING

60g unsalted butter, cubed

120g plain flour

1 tablespoon caster sugar

FOR THE BUTTERCREAM ICING

300g unsalted butter, softened

675g icing sugar

1 x cherry **fruit goo** (see page 34)

YOU NEED

2 x 12-hole muffin trays,
with snug-fitting paper cases

1 x piping bag (with 5mm nozzle)

Preheat the oven to 170°C fan/375°F/gas 5. For the pie crumble topping, melt the butter in a small pan over a low heat, then pour it into a large bowl. Add the remaining crumble ingredients, 1 pinch of fine sea salt and ¾ of a tablespoon of water and beat until the mixture comes together into little clumps. Tip onto a baking tray lined with greaseproof paper, spread out evenly and bake for 20 minutes, or until lightly golden.

Meanwhile, place the ground almonds in a large bowl, then sift in the remaining dry cupcake ingredients (apart from the flaked almonds). Add the butter and eggs, then beat for 60 seconds with an electric mixer (I prefer the free-standing type). Stir the almond extract into the milk, then add to the mix and beat for 20 seconds, or until well combined. Scrape down the sides of the bowl with a spatula, then give the mix a final blast for 30 seconds to make sure it's all incorporated. Fill the paper cases two-thirds full with mixture, but don't bother to smooth it out. Bake for 20 minutes, or until they spring back when touched. Leave to cool, transferring to a wire cooling rack after 5 minutes.

Meanwhile, toast the flaked almonds in a pan over a high heat for 1 to 2 minutes, tossing often until golden, then leave to cool. For the icing, beat the butter for 4 to 5 minutes, or until pale and smooth. Sift the icing sugar into a large bowl, then add to the butter in two stages, beating well between each. Gradually add 5 tablespoons of the cherry **fruit goo** and beat for a further 3 to 5 minutes, or until well combined. Have a taste – if the cherry flavour isn't strong enough, add a couple of drops of almond extract to enhance it.

Once the cupcakes are cool, poke a hole into the middle of each with a chopstick, twist to widen the hole, then use a piping bag to fill each one with a little cherry fruit goo. Decorate each cake with a swirl of piped icing, sprinkle with the toasted almonds and pie crumble topping and enjoy.

Cardamom & white chocolate cupcakes

MAKES 24

TOTAL TIME: 50 MINUTES
PLUS COOLING

FOR THE CUPCAKES

250g self-raising flour

250g caster sugar

½ teaspoon bicarbonate of soda

250g unsalted butter, softened

4 large free-range eggs

3 tablespoons cardamom
infused milk (see page 32)

FOR THE BUTTERCREAM ICING

180g white chocolate, broken into
chunks, or white chocolate chips

300g unsalted butter, softened

540g icing sugar

4 tablespoons whole milk

YOU NEED

2 x 12-hole muffin trays,
with snug-fitting paper cases

Preheat the oven to 170°C fan/375°F/gas 5. Sift the dry cupcake ingredients into a large bowl, add the butter and eggs, then beat for 60 seconds with an electric mixer (I prefer the free-standing type). Pour in the cardamom **infused milk** and beat for 20 seconds, or until well combined. Scrape down the sides of the bowl with a spatula, then give the mix a final blast for 30 seconds to make sure it's all incorporated. Fill the paper cases two-thirds full with mixture, but don't bother to smooth it out. Bake for 20 minutes, or until they spring back when touched. Leave to cool, transferring to a wire cooling rack after 5 minutes.

Meanwhile, make the icing. Melt the chocolate in a heatproof bowl over a pan of simmering water, making sure the base doesn't touch the water, then leave to cool for 5 to 10 minutes – the bowl should be just cool enough to handle. While it's cooling, beat the butter with an electric mixer for 4 to 5 minutes, or until pale and smooth. Sift the icing sugar into a large bowl, then add to the butter in two stages, beating well between each. Gradually add the milk and beat for a further 3 to 5 minutes, or until well combined. Pour in the melted chocolate, bit by bit, mixing as you go, then beat for a couple of minutes, or until the icing is silky smooth. Once the cupcakes are cool, decorate them with the icing and enjoy with a nice cup of coffee.

To make these extra classy, I sometimes like to top them with a slice or two of crystallized ginger or a shaving of white chocolate.

Raspberry & coconut cupcakes

TOTAL TIME: 1 HOUR 10 MINUTES PLUS COOLING

FOR THE CUPCAKES

120g desiccated coconut, plus extra for decorating

250g self-raising flour

250g caster sugar

½ teaspoon bicarbonate of soda

250g unsalted butter, softened

4 large free-range eggs

3 tablespoons whole milk

3 tablespoons raspberry **fruit goo** (see page 34)

FOR THE BUTTERCREAM ICING

300g unsalted butter, softened

675g icing sugar

5 tablespoons coconut cream

YOU NEED

2 x 12-hole muffin trays, with snug-fitting paper cases

Preheat the oven to 170°C fan/375°F/gas 5, then place the coconut on a baking tray and lightly toast in the oven for 3 to 5 minutes. Sift the remaining dry cupcake ingredients into a large bowl and add the toasted coconut, butter and eggs, then beat for 60 seconds with an electric mixer (I prefer the free-standing type). Pour in the milk and whisk for another 20 seconds, or until well combined. Scrape down the sides of the bowl with a spatula, then give the mix a final blast for 30 seconds to make sure it's all incorporated.

Swirl the raspberry **fruit goo** through the cupcake mix to create a rippled effect, then fill the paper cases two-thirds full with mixture, but don't bother to smooth it out. Bake for 20 minutes, or until they spring back when touched. Leave to cool, transferring to a wire cooling rack after 5 minutes.

Meanwhile, make the icing. Beat the butter with an electric mixer for 4 to 5 minutes, or until pale and smooth. Sift the icing sugar into a large bowl, then add to the butter in two stages, beating well between each. Add the coconut cream and beat for a further 3 to 5 minutes, or until well combined – if the icing is a little stiff, add a drop more coconut cream and whisk again. Once the cupcakes are cool, decorate them with the icing. Dip each cupcake into some extra desiccated coconut so they're nicely covered, and if you've got any leftover raspberry fruit goo, drizzle that on top too, then serve.

One whiff of coconut and I'm transported to a tropical beach. Sadly the beach is a mere figment of my overworked imagination, but who cares when there are raspberry and coconut cupcakes on offer?

Autumn

The leaves are changing colour, the wind is blowing and the heating is going on – cakes to warm you from the inside.

Banoffee pie cupcakes

✳ ✳ ✳ **MAKES 24** ✳ ✳ ✳

TOTAL TIME: 1 HOUR 15 MINUTES
PLUS COOLING

FOR THE CUPCAKES

400g unsalted butter, cubed

175g soft dark brown sugar

1 x 397g tin of sweetened
condensed milk

200g caster sugar

280g self-raising flour

¾ teaspoon bicarbonate of soda

4 large free-range eggs

1 very ripe banana, peeled

2 tablespoons whole milk

FOR THE BUTTERY BISCUIT BASE

50g unsalted butter, cubed

175g digestive biscuits

1 tablespoon golden syrup

FOR THE BUTTERCREAM ICING

300g unsalted butter, softened

540g icing sugar

1–2 tablespoons whole milk

YOU NEED

2 x 12-hole muffin trays,
with snug-fitting paper cases

1 x piping bag (with 5mm nozzle)

Preheat the oven to 170°C fan/375°F/gas 5. For the cupcakes, put 150g of butter and 150g of brown sugar into a small pan over a medium heat and stir continuously until the sugar dissolves. Add the condensed milk and bring to the boil, then cook on a low heat for 3 to 4 minutes, or until dark golden, stirring continuously to make toffee. Leave to cool.

For the buttery biscuit base, melt the butter in a small pan over a low heat, then blitz the biscuits to fine crumbs in a food processor. Combine both with the golden syrup, then scoop 1 tablespoon of the mixture into each paper case, pressing down to make a nice firm base. Whisk the remaining sugars for the cupcakes in a large bowl with an electric mixer (I prefer the free-standing type) to get rid of any lumps, then sift in the remaining dry cupcake ingredients. Add the remaining 250g of butter (softened) and the eggs, mash and add the banana, then beat for 60 seconds. Pour in the milk and beat for 20 seconds, or until well combined. Scrape down the sides of the bowl with a spatula, then give the mix a final blast for 30 seconds to make sure it's all incorporated. Fill the paper cases two-thirds full with mixture, but don't bother to smooth it out. Bake for 20 minutes, or until they spring back when touched. Leave to cool, transferring to a wire cooling rack after 5 minutes.

Meanwhile, make the icing. Beat the butter with an electric mixer for 4 to 5 minutes, or until pale and smooth. Sift the icing sugar into a large bowl, then add to the butter in two stages, beating well between each. Add half the toffee and beat for a further 3 to 5 minutes, gradually adding the milk until smooth and silky. Once the cupcakes are cool, poke a hole into the middle of each with a chopstick, twist to widen the hole, then use a piping bag to fill each one with a little toffee. Decorate the cakes with the icing and a drizzle of the remaining toffee. I like to add a shaving or two of dark chocolate, too. This is one of the most satisfying flavours to make it on to the Crumbs & Doilies menu.

Spiced pumpkin cupcakes

MAKES
24

TOTAL TIME: 45 MINUTES
PLUS COOLING

FOR THE CUPCAKES

220g caster sugar

175g soft dark brown sugar

300g self-raising flour

½ teaspoon bicarbonate of soda

2 teaspoons ground cinnamon

1 teaspoon ground ginger

1 teaspoon ground nutmeg

1 x 425g tin of unsweetened
pumpkin purée

200ml vegetable oil

4 large free-range eggs

50g pumpkin seeds

FOR THE CREAM CHEESE ICING

1 x **cream cheese icing**
(see page 20)

YOU NEED

2 x 12-hole muffin trays,
with snug-fitting paper cases

Preheat the oven to 170°C fan/375°F/gas 5. Whisk the sugars in a large bowl with an electric mixer (I prefer the free-standing type) to get rid of any lumps, then sift in the remaining dry cupcake ingredients (apart from the pumkin seeds), and 1 teaspoon of fine sea salt. Whisk the wet cupcake ingredients together in a bowl, then add to the dry mix, beating until smooth and glossy. Fill the paper cases two-thirds full with mixture, but don't bother to smooth it out. Bake for 20 minutes, or until they spring back when touched. Leave to cool, transferring to a wire cooling rack after 5 minutes.

Meanwhile, gently toast the pumpkin seeds in a pan over a high heat for 1 to 2 minutes, tossing often until golden and starting to pop, then set aside to cool. Once the cupcakes are cool, decorate them with the **cream cheese icing**, then roughly chop the toasted seeds and sprinkle on top.

This may be the easiest recipe in the book, but boy, it's good! These cupcakes are soft and fudgy, with the autumnal flavours of pumpkin, cinnamon and ginger.

PB & J cupcakes

  MAKES 24

TOTAL TIME: 50 MINUTES
PLUS COOLING

FOR THE CUPCAKES

250g self-raising flour

250g caster sugar

½ teaspoon bicarbonate of soda

270g unsalted butter, softened

4 large free-range eggs

100g peanut butter

2 tablespoons whole milk

¾ x 340g jar of quality
seedless raspberry jam

FOR THE PEANUT CRUMB

100g peanut butter

100g icing sugar

FOR THE BUTTERCREAM ICING

300g unsalted butter, softened

120g peanut butter

540g icing sugar

4 tablespoons whole milk

YOU NEED

2 x 12-hole muffin trays,
with snug-fitting paper cases

1 x piping bag (with 5mm nozzle)

Preheat the oven to 170°C fan/375°F/gas 5. Sift the dry cupcake ingredients and 1 pinch of fine sea salt into a large bowl, add the butter, eggs and peanut butter, then beat for 60 seconds with an electric mixer (I prefer the free-standing type). Pour in the milk and whisk for 20 seconds, or until well combined. Scrape down the sides of the bowl with a spatula, then give the mix a final blast for 30 seconds to make sure it's all incorporated. Fill the paper cases two-thirds full with mixture, but don't bother to smooth it out. Bake for 20 minutes, or until they spring back when touched. Leave to cool slightly, transferring to a wire cooling rack after 5 minutes.

Meanwhile, make the peanut crumb. Place the peanut butter in a food processor, sift in the icing sugar and whiz for 1 to 2 minutes to make small, delicious crumbs, then set aside.

For the icing, beat the butter and peanut butter with an electric mixer for 5 to 6 minutes, or until pale and fluffy. Sift the icing sugar into a large bowl, then add to the butter in two stages, beating well between each. Pour in the milk and beat for a further 3 to 5 minutes, or until well combined. Once the cupcakes are cool, poke a hole into the middle of each with a chopstick, twist to widen the hole, then use a piping bag to fill each one with a good squeeze of jam. Decorate with the icing, top with a blob of jam or a drizzle of raspberry **fruit goo** (see page 34), if you like, and a sprinkling of peanut crumb to finish, then enjoy.

> Turning classic treats into cupcakes is one of my favourite things to do and this is the star of the show. Feel free to use smooth or crunchy peanut butter – whichever you prefer.

Malteser cupcakes

MAKES 24

FOR THE CUPCAKES

50g Horlicks original malt

2 teaspoons cocoa powder

190g self-raising flour

½ teaspoon bicarbonate of soda

250g caster sugar

280g unsalted butter, softened

4 large free-range eggs

3 tablespoons whole milk

FOR THE BUTTERCREAM ICING

300g unsalted butter, softened

1 tablespoon Horlicks original malt

4 tablespoons whole milk

675g icing sugar

100g Maltesers, plus extra
for decorating

YOU NEED

2 x 12-hole muffin trays,
with snug-fitting paper cases

Preheat the oven to 170°C fan/375°F/gas 5. Sift the dry cupcake ingredients and 1 pinch of fine sea salt into a large bowl, add the butter and eggs, then beat for 60 seconds with an electric mixer (I prefer the free-standing type). Add the milk and beat for 20 seconds, or until well combined. Scrape down the sides of the bowl with a spatula, then give the mix a final blast for 30 seconds to make sure it's all incorporated. Fill the paper cases two-thirds full with mixture, but don't bother to smooth it out. Bake for 20 minutes, or until they spring back when touched. Leave to cool, transferring to a wire cooling rack after 5 minutes.

Meanwhile, make the icing. Beat the butter with an electric mixer for 4 to 5 minutes, or until pale and smooth. Stir the Horlicks into the milk and set aside. Sift the icing sugar into a large bowl, then add to the butter in two stages, beating well between each. Add the Horlicks milk and beat for a further 3 to 5 minutes, or until smooth. Wrap the Maltesers in a clean tea towel and bash to fine crumbs with a rolling pin, then fold through the icing. Once the cupcakes are cool, decorate them with the icing – it won't be completely smooth, so don't worry if they look rustic. Top with whole or crushed Maltesers, and enjoy.

Jamaican ginger cake

SERVES 16

TOTAL TIME: 1 HOUR 15 MINUTES
PLUS COOLING

FOR THE SPONGE

375g unsalted butter, plus extra
for greasing, softened

330g soft dark brown sugar

225g black treacle

75g golden syrup

6 large free-range eggs

375g self-raising flour

4 tablespoons ground ginger

3 teaspoons ground cinnamon

4½ tablespoons soured cream

8 pieces of jarred stem ginger
and 6 tablespoons syrup

FOR THE ICING

1 x **cream cheese icing**
(see page 20)

YOU NEED

3 x 20cm sandwich cake tins,
greased and lined

Preheat the oven to 170°C fan/375°F/gas 5. Place the butter, sugar, treacle and golden syrup into a large bowl, then beat with an electric mixer (I prefer the free-standing type) for 5 to 7 minutes, or until light and fluffy. Crack in the eggs one at a time, whisking well before adding the next – if the mixture starts to split, whisk in 1 tablespoon of the flour. Sift in the ground ginger, cinnamon and flour and fold through, then stir in the soured cream. Strain the ginger syrup into a bowl and set aside, chop the ginger into 0.5cm pieces, then stir them into the cake mixture.

Equally divide the mixture between the prepared cake tins, smoothing it out with a spatula. Bake the cakes for 25 minutes, or until an inserted skewer comes out clean, then turn them out on to a wire cooling rack and leave to cool.

Once the cakes have cooled, use a sharp serrated knife to trim the tops off them to make the surfaces nice and flat. Generously brush some ginger syrup over a flat round and spread with some of the **cream cheese icing**. Layer over another sponge, top with another layer of ginger syrup and icing, then finish with the remaining sponge. Use a palette knife to smooth the sides and the top of the cake with the rest of the icing, finish with an extra drizzle of ginger syrup, et voilà!

> I sometimes like to sprinkle the top with crushed ginger biscuits and extra pieces of stem or crystallized ginger, or even get creative and decorate the edges like I've done in the picture, but it's up to you. Go nuts!

Mexican hot chocolate cupcakes

**TOTAL TIME: 45 MINUTES
PLUS COOLING**

FOR THE CUPCAKES

35g ground almonds

170g self-raising flour

250g caster sugar

½ teaspoon bicarbonate of soda

35g cocoa powder

1 teaspoon chilli powder

1 teaspoon ground cinnamon

250g unsalted butter, softened

4 large free-range eggs

½ teaspoon vanilla extract

3 tablespoons whole milk

chilli flakes, for decorating

FOR THE BUTTERCREAM ICING

180g dark chocolate (70%)

1 tablespoon chilli powder

1 tablespoon ground cinnamon

300g unsalted butter, softened

540g icing sugar

4 tablespoons whole milk

YOU NEED

2 x 12-hole muffin trays,
with snug-fitting paper cases

Preheat the oven to 170°C fan/375°F/gas 5. Place the ground almonds in a large bowl, then sift in the remaining dry cupcake ingredients and 1 pinch of fine sea salt and whisk with an electric mixer (I prefer the free-standing type). Add the butter and eggs, then beat for 60 seconds. Stir the vanilla extract into the milk, then add to the mix and beat for 20 seconds, or until well combined. Scrape down the sides of the bowl with a spatula, then give the mix a final blast for 30 seconds to make sure it's all incorporated. Fill the paper cases two-thirds full with mixture, but don't bother to smooth it out. Bake for 20 minutes, or until they spring back when touched. Leave to cool, transferring to a wire cooling rack after 5 minutes.

Meanwhile, make the icing. Melt the chocolate in a heatproof bowl with the chilli powder and cinnamon over a pan of simmering water, making sure the base doesn't touch the water, then leave to cool for 5 to 10 minutes – the bowl should be just cool enough to handle. While it's cooling, beat the butter with an electric mixer for 4 to 5 minutes, or until pale and smooth. Sift the icing sugar into a large bowl, then add to the butter in two stages, beating well between each. Add the milk and beat for a further 5 minutes, or until well combined. Pour in the melted chilli chocolate bit by bit, mixing as you go, then beat for a couple of minutes, or until the icing is a rich chocolate-brown colour. Once the cupcakes are cool, decorate them with the icing and some chilli flakes for an extra kick.

> There are all sorts of varieties of dried chilli flakes available in the shops – see what you can find and experiment with different flavours to find your favourite chilli-chocolate combo.

Buttered popcorn cupcakes

MAKES
24

TOTAL TIME: 1 HOUR 30 MINUTES
PLUS COOLING

FOR THE CUPCAKES

275g unsalted butter, cubed

130g caster sugar

120g soft dark brown sugar

250g self-raising flour

½ teaspoon bicarbonate of soda

4 large free-range eggs

3 tablespoons whole milk

30g salted popcorn

FOR THE BUTTERCREAM ICING

300g unsalted butter, softened

535g icing sugar

1 x **salted caramel** (see page 28)

YOU NEED

2 x 12-hole muffin trays,
with snug-fitting paper cases

Preheat the oven to 170°C fan/375°F/gas 5. For the cupcakes, place 200g of butter into a pan over a medium heat and cook for 5 to 6 minutes, or until rich and golden in colour, stirring continuously. Transfer to a heatproof bowl and leave to cool, then place in the fridge for 15 to 20 minutes, or until set to a spreadable consistency, stirring occasionally. Whisk the sugars in a large bowl with an electric whisk (I prefer the free-standing type) to get rid of any lumps, then sift in the remaining dry cupcake ingredients (apart from the popcorn), and 1 pinch of fine sea salt. Add the burnt butter, eggs and the remaining 75g of butter (softened), then beat for 60 seconds. Pour in the milk and whisk for 20 seconds, or until well combined. Scrape down the sides with a spatula, then give the mix a final blast for 30 seconds to make sure it's all incorporated. Fill the paper cases two-thirds full with mixture, but don't bother to smooth it out. Bake for 20 minutes, or until they spring back when touched. Leave to cool, transferring to a wire cooling rack after 5 minutes.

Meanwhile, make the icing. Beat the butter with an electric mixer for 4 to 5 minutes, or until pale and smooth. Sift the icing sugar into a large bowl with ½ a tablespoon of fine sea salt, then add to the butter in two stages, beating well between each. Gradually add half the **salted caramel**, then beat for a further 3 to 5 minutes, or until smooth. Once the cupcakes are cool, decorate them with the icing and sprinkle with popcorn, gently pressing it in so it sticks. Drizzle over the remaining salted caramel to finish and enjoy.

> Feel free to buy packs of microwaveable popcorn, or make your own from scratch, with a little oil and butter and a sprinkling of salt to finish.

Bonfire cupcakes

✳ ✳ ✳ ⬤ MAKES 24 ✳ ✳ ✳

TOTAL TIME: 1 HOUR 5 MINUTES
PLUS COOLING

FOR THE CUPCAKES

250ml Guinness original stout

250g unsalted butter, cubed

70g cocoa powder

400g caster sugar

2 large free-range eggs

1 teaspoon vanilla extract

140ml soured cream

225g plain flour

2½ teaspoons bicarbonate of soda

½ teaspoon ancho chilli powder

FOR THE MERINGUE ICING

1 x **marshmallowy meringue icing**
(see page 26)

yellow, orange and red
food-colouring pastes

YOU NEED

2 x 12-hole muffin trays,
with snug-fitting paper cases

1 x large piping bag
(with 1cm star-shaped nozzle)

optional: 1 x blowtorch

Preheat the oven to 170°C fan/375°F/gas 5. Place the Guinness and butter in a pan over a medium heat and allow the butter to melt, but make sure it doesn't boil. Add the cocoa powder and sugar and whisk until dissolved, then remove from the heat and allow to cool slightly.

Crack the eggs into a large bowl, add the vanilla extract and soured cream and beat with an electric mixer (I prefer the free-standing type) until well combined. Gradually pour in the Guinness mixture, whisking continuously, then mix in the remaining cupcake ingredients and 1 pinch of fine sea salt, beating constantly until silky smooth. Transfer the mixture to a small jug (you'll need to do this in batches), and carefully fill the paper cases just over two-thirds full. Bake for 20 minutes, or until they spring back when touched. Leave to cool, transferring to a wire cooling rack after 5 minutes.

Meanwhile, equally divide the **marshmallowy meringue icing** between three bowls. Mix a pea-sized blob of each food-colouring paste into each bowl. Fill a piping bag with the different icings, layering them up to create a swirling rainbow effect. Once the cupcakes are cool, carefully pipe swirly blobs of the icing on to them, so each cake has a tower of different colours, and enjoy.

These cupcakes are so much fun to make – they look just like little bonfires! If you have a blowtorch, lightly toast the icing on a heatproof surface, until the tips are slightly burnt. The other thing I sometimes like to do if you want to go all out, is to mix 1 heaped teaspoon of chocolate-coated popping candy into each batch of icing, along with the food-colouring paste.

Toffee apple cupcakes

MAKES
24

TOTAL TIME: 55 MINUTES
PLUS COOLING

FOR THE CUPCAKES

2 x 150g Cox's apples or 1 x 300g
Bramley apple, peeled and cored

250g self-raising flour

½ teaspoon bicarbonate of soda

250g caster sugar

250g unsalted butter, softened

4 large free-range eggs

2 tablespoons black treacle

FOR THE APPLE CARAMEL

3 x 150g Cox's apples,
peeled and cored

75g unsalted butter, cubed

150g soft dark brown sugar

140ml double cream

FOR THE BUTTERCREAM ICING

375g unsalted butter, softened

530g icing sugar

YOU NEED

2 x 12-hole muffin trays,
with snug-fitting paper cases

1 x piping bag (with 5mm nozzle)

Preheat the oven to 170°C fan/375°F/gas 5. For the cupcakes, coarsely grate the apples, then put them in a sieve and use the back of a spoon to push the juice through into a bowl, then set aside. Place the pulp into a large bowl, then mix in the dry cupcake ingredients. Add the butter and eggs, then beat for 60 seconds with an electric mixer (I prefer the free-standing type). Add the treacle and 3 tablespoons of the apple juice, then whisk for another 20 seconds, or until well combined. Scrape down the sides of the bowl with a spatula, then give the mix a final blast for 30 seconds to make sure it's all incorporated. Fill the paper cases two-thirds full with mixture, but don't bother to smooth it out. Bake for 20 minutes, or until they spring back when touched. Leave to cool, transferring to a wire cooling rack after 5 minutes.

Meanwhile, make the apple caramel. Coarsely grate the apples into a pan and place over a high heat. Add the butter and brown sugar and bring to the boil, then reduce to a simmer for 5 to 6 minutes, or until it deepens in colour, stirring occasionally. Remove from the heat, slowly pour in the cream, stirring continuously, then allow to cool completely.

To make the icing, beat the butter with an electric mixer for 4 to 5 minutes, or until pale and smooth. Sift the icing sugar into a large bowl, then add to the butter in two stages, beating well between each. Pour in just over half of the apple caramel and beat for a further 3 to 5 minutes, or until combined and fairly smooth. Once the cupcakes are cool, poke a hole into the middle of each with a chopstick, twist to widen the hole, then use a piping bag to fill each one with apple caramel. Decorate with the icing and enjoy. Sometimes I like to add a few homemade dried apple slices too.

Caramel mudslide cupcakes

FOR THE CUPCAKES

185g unsalted butter, cubed

185g dark chocolate (70%)

1½ tablespoons instant
coffee granules

3 large free-range eggs

2 tablespoons vegetable oil

105ml buttermilk

110g self-raising flour

110g plain flour

45g cocoa powder

½ teaspoon bicarbonate of soda

310g caster sugar

FOR THE BUTTERCREAM ICING

300g unsalted butter, softened

535g icing sugar

1 x **salted caramel** (see page 28)

YOU NEED

2 x 12-hole muffin trays,
with snug-fitting paper cases

1 x piping bag (with 5mm nozzle)

Preheat the oven to 170°C fan/375°F/gas 5. For the cupcakes, warm the butter, chocolate, coffee and 135ml of water in a pan over a low heat until smooth, stirring occasionally. Set aside to cool.

Place the remaining wet cupcake ingredients in a large bowl and whisk together with an electric mixer (I prefer the free-standing type). Add the cooled chocolate mixture and beat until well combined. Mix the remaining cupcake ingredients in a bowl and add to the mixture, beating continuously until silky smooth. Transfer the mixture to a small jug (you'll need to do this in batches) and carefully fill the paper cases just over two-thirds full. Bake for 20 minutes, or until they spring back when touched. Leave to cool, transferring to a wire cooling rack after 5 minutes.

Meanwhile, make the icing. Beat the butter with an electric mixer for 4 to 5 minutes, or until pale and smooth. Sift the icing sugar and ½ a tablespoon of fine sea salt into a large bowl, then add to the butter in two stages, beating well between each. Gradually add half the **salted caramel**, then beat for a further 3 to 5 minutes, or until smooth. Once the cupcakes are cool, poke a hole into the middle of each with a chopstick, twist to widen the hole, then use a piping bag to fill each one with a good squeeze of salted caramel. Decorate with the icing and an extra drizzling of salted caramel, if you're feeling decadent, or top them off with a few of your favourite sprinkles, if you like.

Despite our best efforts, none of us here at Crumbs & Doilies has ever been able to finish more than one of these rich, decadent and ridiculously indulgent cupcakes.

Winter

Indulge, celebrate, get cosy, wrap up warm
cakes for sharing or for keeping all to yourself.

Hot toddy cupcakes

MAKES
24

TOTAL TIME: 45 MINUTES
PLUS COOLING

FOR THE CUPCAKES

245g self-raising flour

250g caster sugar

½ teaspoon bicarbonate of soda

1 heaped teaspoon
ground cinnamon

¼ teaspoon ground cloves

270g unsalted butter, softened

4 large free-range eggs

zest from 2 unwaxed lemons and
3 tablespoons lemon juice

3 tablespoons whole milk

FOR THE BUTTERCREAM ICING
& HOT TODDY SYRUP

300g unsalted butter, softened

675g icing sugar

3 tablespoons runny honey

85ml lemon juice (4 lemons)

5½ tablespoons whisky

100g caster sugar

5 cloves

YOU NEED

2 x 12-hole muffin trays,
with snug-fitting paper cases

Preheat the oven to 170°C fan/375°F/gas 5. Sift the dry cupcake ingredients into a large bowl, add the butter, eggs, lemon zest and juice, then beat for 60 seconds with an electric mixer (I prefer the free-standing type). Pour in the milk and beat for 20 seconds, or until well combined. Scrape down the sides of the bowl with a spatula, then give the mix a final blast for 30 seconds to make sure it's all incorporated. Fill the paper cases two-thirds full with mixture, but don't bother to smooth it out. Bake for 20 minutes, or until they spring back when touched. Leave to cool, transferring to a wire cooling rack after 5 minutes.

Meanwhile, make the icing. Beat the butter with an electric mixer for 4 to 5 minutes, or until pale and smooth. Sift the icing sugar into a large bowl, then add to the butter in two stages, beating well between each. Add 2 tablespoons of honey, ¾ of a tablespoon of lemon juice and 4 tablespoons of whisky and beat for a further 3 to 5 minutes, or until combined, then set aside.

For the hot toddy syrup, place the caster sugar, 1 tablespoon of honey, 75ml of lemon juice, 1½ tablespoons of whisky and the cloves in a pan over a medium heat. Cook for 5 to 8 minutes, or until thick and syrupy but not coloured, swirling the pan occasionally. Pour through a sieve into a bowl and leave to cool slightly. Once the cupcakes are cool, decorate them with the icing, leaving a little well in the middle for the hot toddy syrup – then drizzle over the syrup and eat immediately.

The hot toddy is the king of hot drinks – it's a soothing pick-me-up beverage with flavour combos that are begging to be cupcaked. These will help slap winter right in the chops!

Jaffa cake

SERVES 16

TOTAL TIME: 1 HOUR 5 MINUTES
PLUS COOLING

FOR THE SPONGE

400g unsalted butter, plus extra
for greasing, softened

300g caster sugar

75g soft dark brown sugar

1 tablespoon black treacle

6 large free-range eggs

320g self-raising flour

50g cocoa powder

3 unwaxed oranges (350g)

3–4 tablespoons whole milk

FOR THE FILLINGS

110g caster sugar

1½ tablespoons agar flakes

1 x **chocolate orange ganache**
(see page 22)

YOU NEED

3 x 20cm sandwich cake tins,
greased and lined

Preheat the oven to 170°C fan/375°F/gas 5. To make the sponge, place the butter, sugars and treacle in a large bowl, then beat with an electric mixer (I prefer the free-standing type) for 5 to 7 minutes, or until light and fluffy. Crack in the eggs one at a time, whisking well before adding the next. Sift the flour and cocoa powder into a separate bowl, then fold into the wet mixture with the zest from the oranges. Pour in the milk and beat until well combined.

Equally divide the mixture between the prepared cake tins, smoothing it out with a spatula. Bake the cakes for 25 minutes, or until an inserted skewer comes out clean, then turn them out on to a wire cooling rack and leave to cool.

Meanwhile, to make the jelly filling peel and roughly chop the oranges and place in a pan over a medium heat, with the sugar and agar flakes. Bring to the boil, then reduce the heat to a simmer for 10 to 15 minutes, or until softened and broken down, occasionally mashing the oranges with a spoon. To check if the jelly is ready, scoop ½ a teaspoon of the mixture on to a cold surface – if it hardens to soft-set jelly, it's ready. Pour through a sieve into a bowl, then leave to cool.

Once the cakes have cooled, use a sharp serrated knife to trim the tops off them to make the surfaces nice and flat. Spread one-third of the **chocolate orange ganache** onto a round, then top with a good layer of jelly. Layer over another sponge, top with one-third of the ganache and another layer of jelly, then finish with the remaining sponge. Use a palette knife to smooth the sides and the top of the cake with the rest of the ganache, then serve.

Chai-spiced cupcakes

MAKES
24

FOR THE CUPCAKES

250g self-raising flour

½ teaspoon bicarbonate of soda

250g caster sugar

½ teaspoon ground cloves

½ teaspoon ground cinnamon

½ teaspoon ground cardamom

250g unsalted butter, softened

4 large free-range eggs

3 tablespoons chai **infused milk**
(see page 32)

FOR THE BUTTERCREAM ICING

300g unsalted butter, softened

675g icing sugar

4 tablespoons chai **infused milk**
(see page 32)

2 tablespoons demerara sugar

1 teaspoon ground cinnamon

¼ teaspoon ground nutmeg

1 pinch of ground cloves

YOU NEED

2 x 12-hole muffin trays,
with snug-fitting paper cases

Preheat the oven to 170°C fan/375°F/gas 5. Sift the dry cupcake ingredients into a large bowl, add the butter and eggs, then beat for 60 seconds with an electric mixer (I prefer the free-standing type). Add the chai **infused milk** and whisk for 20 seconds, or until well combined. Scrape down the sides of the bowl with a spatula, then give the mix a final blast for 30 seconds to make sure it's incorporated. Fill the paper cases two-thirds full with mixture, but don't bother to smooth it out. Bake for 20 minutes, or until they spring back when touched. Leave to cool, transferring to a wire cooling rack after 5 minutes.

Meanwhile, make the icing. Beat the butter with an electric mixer for 4 to 5 minutes, or until pale and smooth. Sift the icing sugar into a bowl, then add to the butter in two stages, beating well between each. Pour in the chai **infused milk** and beat for a further 3 to 5 minutes, or until well combined. Once the cupcakes are cool, decorate them with the icing, then mix the demerara sugar with the spices and sprinkle over the top. Brew yourself a pot of hot chai tea, grab a warm blanket and get cosy.

On a cold night at home, it's not all about hot cocoa. Occasionally something a little more exotic beckons, and in my house that comes in the form of a big old mug of milky chai tea, which is the inspiration behind these lovely things.

Cookies & cream cupcakes

MAKES 24

TOTAL TIME: 1 HOUR 10 MINUTES
PLUS COOLING

FOR THE CUPCAKES

100g dark chocolate (70%)

200g plain flour

120g caster sugar

¾ teaspoon bicarbonate of soda

15g Horlicks original malt

20g cocoa powder

2 large free-range eggs

160ml coffee, cooled (see tip below)

160ml buttermilk

140ml vegetable oil

100ml double cream

FOR THE BUTTERY COOKIE BASE
& BUTTERCREAM ICING

140g unsalted butter, cubed

410g cream-filled cookies

2 tablespoons golden syrup

1 x **vanilla buttercream icing**
(see page 16)

YOU NEED

2 x 12-hole muffin trays,
with snug-fitting paper cases

1 x piping bag (with 5mm nozzle)

Preheat the oven to 160°C fan/350°F/gas 4. For the buttery cookie base, melt the butter over a low heat, then blitz 300g of cookies to fine crumbs in a food processor. Combine both with the golden syrup, then scoop 1 tablespoon of the mixture into each paper case, pressing down to make a nice firm base.

For the cupcakes, finely chop the chocolate (this is best done in a food processor), then tip into a large bowl. Sift in the remaining dry cupcake ingredients and ½ a teaspoon of fine sea salt, then stir to combine. Whisk the wet cupcake ingredients (apart from the cream) in a separate bowl with an electric mixer (I prefer the free-standing type), then gradually add to the dry mix until silky smooth. Transfer the mixture to a small jug (you'll need to do this in batches) and carefully fill the paper cases just over two-thirds full. Bake for 20 minutes, or until they spring back when touched. Leave to cool, transferring to a wire cooling rack after 5 minutes.

Meanwhile, whisk the double cream with 1 heaped teaspoon of caster sugar until soft peaks form. Scoop into a piping bag and place in the fridge, until needed. Once the cupcakes are cool, poke a hole into the middle of each with a chopstick, twist to widen the hole, then use a piping bag to fill each one with a good squeeze of the sweetened cream. For the icing, crush the remaining 110g of cookies to fine crumbs, then fold most of them through the **vanilla buttercream icing**. Decorate the cupcakes with the icing, sprinkle over the remaining crushed cookies (or try decorating with whole cookies, wodged into the buttercream, for an extra decadent finish), and serve with a glass of milk.

> If you don't have freshly brewed coffee, simply mix ½ a tablespoon of instant coffee with 160ml of hot water instead.

Ridiculous chocolate cake

SERVES 16

TOTAL TIME: 1 HOUR 30 MINUTES
PLUS COOLING

FOR THE SPONGES

350g plain flour

65g cocoa powder

570g caster sugar

1 teaspoon bicarbonate of soda

240ml coffee, cooled
(see tip page 112)

240ml buttermilk

210ml vegetable oil

7 large free-range eggs

270g unsalted butter

50g soft dark brown sugar

250g self-raising flour

¼ teaspoon vanilla extract

3 tablespoons whole milk

FOR THE FILLING & ICING

300g unsalted butter, softened

530g icing sugar

1 x **salted caramel** (see page 28)

½ x **chocolate ganache**
(see page 22)

salted pretzels, broken

YOU NEED

4 x 20cm sandwich cake tins,
greased and lined

Preheat the oven to 170°C fan/375°F/gas 5. To make the chocolate sponge, sift the plain flour and cocoa powder into a large bowl, along with 370g of caster sugar, the bicarbonate of soda and ½ a teaspoon of salt, then whisk with an electric mixer (I prefer the free-standing type) to combine. Mix the coffee, buttermilk, oil and 3 eggs together in a bowl, then add to the dry mix, whisking until smooth. Equally divide the mixture between two prepared cake tins, smoothing it out with a spatula. Bake the cakes for 25 minutes, or until an inserted skewer comes out clean, then turn them out on to a wire cooling rack and leave to cool.

Next, make the salted caramel sponge by beating the butter, brown sugar, remaining 200g caster sugar and a pinch of salt with an electric mixer for 5 to 7 minutes, or until pale and fluffy. Crack in the remaining 4 eggs, one at a time, whisking well before adding the next. Sift the self-raising flour into the mixture and fold through. Stir the vanilla extract into the milk, then pour into the mix. Equally divide the mixture between the remaining two prepared cake tins, smoothing it out with a spatula. Bake the cakes for 20 minutes, or until an inserted skewer comes out clean, then turn them out on to a wire cooling rack and leave to cool.

For the filling, beat the butter with an electric mixer for 4 minutes, or until pale and smooth. Sift the icing sugar and ½ a tablespoon of salt into a large bowl, then add to the butter in two stages, beating well between each. Gradually add just over half the **salted caramel** and beat for a further 3 to 5 minutes, or until smooth. Once the cakes have cooled, use a sharp serrated knife to trim the tops off them to make the surfaces nice and flat, then carefully halve each sponge horizontally so you end up with eight rounds. Spread one-eighth of the buttercream onto a chocolate sponge, drizzle with salted caramel, top with a salted caramel sponge and more fillings, then repeat. Use a palette knife to smooth the sides and the top of the cake with the **chocolate ganache**, sprinkle with pretzels and more salted caramel.

Cinnamon toast cupcakes

MAKES 24

TOTAL TIME: 1 HOUR 5 MINUTES
PLUS COOLING

FOR THE CUPCAKES

4 slices of brown bread

270g unsalted butter, plus extra
for spreading, softened

225g caster sugar

25g soft dark brown sugar

200g self-raising flour

½ teaspoon bicarbonate of soda

1½ teaspoons ground cinnamon

4 large free-range eggs

2 tablespoons whole milk

FOR THE BUTTERCREAM ICING

300g unsalted butter, softened

675g icing sugar

ground cinnamon

4 tablespoons whole milk

4 tablespoons granulated sugar

YOU NEED

2 x 12-hole muffin trays,
with snug-fitting paper cases

Preheat the oven to 170°C fan/375°F/gas 5. Toast the bread until slightly burnt, then butter both sides and bake in the oven for 5 to 10 minutes, or until crisp enough to snap. Remove and leave to cool, then whiz in a food processor or grate with a box grater and set aside.

For the cupcakes, whisk the sugars in a large bowl with an electric mixer (I prefer the free-standing type) to get rid of any lumps, then sift in the remaining dry cupcake ingredients. Add the eggs, butter and 50g of the buttered toast crumbs, then beat for 60 seconds. Pour in the milk and whisk for 20 seconds, or until well combined. Scrape down the sides of the bowl with a spatula, then give the mix a final blast for 30 seconds to make sure it's all incorporated. Fill the paper cases two-thirds full with mixture, but don't bother to smooth it out. Bake for 20 minutes, or until they spring back when touched. Leave to cool, transferring to a wire cooling rack after 5 minutes.

Meanwhile, make the icing. Beat the butter with an electric mixer for 4 to 5 minutes, or until pale and smooth. Sift the icing sugar and ½ a teaspoon of cinnamon into a large bowl, then add to the butter in two stages, beating well between each. Pour in the milk and beat for a further 3 to 5 minutes, or until smooth and silky. Once the cupcakes are cool, decorate with the icing and scatter the remaining toast crumbs on top. Combine the granulated sugar with a pinch of cinnamon, then sprinkle over the cupcakes and serve.

This is one of my favourite flavour combos – transforming this breakfast classic into a cupcake works so well, you'll find yourself wanting them for breakfast, lunch and dinner.

Banana, maple & pecan cupcakes

TOTAL TIME: 1 HOUR
PLUS COOLING

FOR THE CUPCAKES

200g caster sugar

25g soft dark brown sugar

280g self-raising flour

¾ teaspoon bicarbonate of soda

250g unsalted butter, softened

4 large free-range eggs

1 very ripe banana, peeled

2 tablespoons whole milk

FOR THE BUTTERCREAM ICING

300g unsalted butter, softened

675g icing sugar

6 tablespoons maple syrup

optional: 1–2 drops
maple extract (see tip below)

FOR THE BRITTLE

1 x pecan **brittle** (see page 30)

YOU NEED

2 x 12-hole muffin trays,
with snug-fitting paper cases

Preheat the oven to 160°C fan/350°F/gas 4. Whisk the sugars in a large bowl with an electric mixer (I prefer the free-standing type) to get rid of any lumps, then sift in the remaining dry cupcake ingredients. Add the butter and eggs, mash and add the banana, then beat for 60 seconds. Pour in the milk and whisk for 20 seconds, or until well combined. Scrape down the sides of the bowl with a spatula, then give the mix a final blast for 30 seconds to make sure it's all incorporated. Fill the paper cases two-thirds full with mixture, but don't bother to smooth it out. Bake for 25 minutes, or until they spring back when touched. Leave to cool, transferring to a wire cooling rack after 5 minutes.

Meanwhile, make the icing. Beat the butter with an electric mixer for 4 to 5 minutes, or until pale and smooth. Sift the icing sugar into a large bowl, then add to the butter in two stages, beating well between each. Add the maple syrup and maple extract (if using), and beat for a further 3 to 5 minutes, or until well combined. Once the cupcakes are cool, decorate them with the icing, then top each one with little chunks of pecan **brittle** and an extra drizzle of maple syrup, if you like.

> If you can find maple extract, adding a couple of drops to the buttercream is a great way to boost the maple flavour without the danger of loosening it too much.

Velvet volcano cupcakes

MAKES
24

TOTAL TIME: 1 HOUR 5 MINUTES
PLUS COOLING

FOR THE CUPCAKES

50g milk chocolate chips

1 x **red velvet cupcakes**
(see page 20)

FOR THE COOKIE DOUGH

25g dark chocolate (70%)

80g plain flour

65g caster sugar

2 tablespoons demerara sugar

85g unsalted butter, softened

1 tablespoon soya yoghurt

1 teaspoon vanilla extract

FOR THE BUTTERY COOKIE BASE
& BUTTERCREAM ICING

70g unsalted butter, cubed

225g cream-filled cookies

1 tablespoon golden syrup

1 x **vanilla buttercream icing**
(see page 16)

100g dark chocolate (70%)

½ x **salted caramel** (see page 28)

YOU NEED

2 x 12-hole muffin trays,
with snug-fitting paper cases

Preheat the oven to 170°C fan/375°F/gas 5. For the cookie dough, finely chop the chocolate (this is best done in a food processor), then tip into a large bowl. Mix in the remaining cookie dough ingredients and ½ a teaspoon of fine sea salt using an electric mixer (I prefer the free-standing type) and beat to a sticky dough. Place on a piece of clingfilm and flatten to roughly 1.5cm thick, then wrap and firm up in the freezer for 2 hours.

For the buttery cookie base, melt the butter in a pan over a low heat, then blitz 150g of cookies to fine crumbs in a food processor. Combine both with the golden syrup, then scoop ½ a tablespoon of the mixture into each paper case, pressing down to make a nice firm base. Pile a teaspoon of milk chocolate chips onto each biscuit base, then fill the cases two-thirds full with the **red velvet cupcake** mix, but don't bother to smooth it out. Chop the frozen cookie dough into 1.5 cm chunks and divide between the cases. Bake for 20 minutes, or until they spring back when touched. Leave to cool, transferring to a wire cooling rack after 5 minutes.

Meanwhile, make the icing. Wrap the remaining 75g of cookies in a clean tea towel and bash with a rolling pin into fine crumbs, then fold most of them through the **vanilla buttercream icing**. Melt the chocolate in a heatproof bowl over a pan of simmering water, making sure the base doesn't touch the water, then leave to cool for 5 to 10 minutes – the bowl should be just cool enough to handle. Once the cupcakes have cooled, decorate them with the icing and drizzle with a generous helping of melted chocolate and **salted caramel**.

> This 'Frankencake' was created by the girls at Crumbs & Doilies when we happened to have loads of leftover bits and bobs. It was so blooming delicious, it quickly became a legendary favourite among our market regulars.

Christmas cupcakes

MAKES 24

TOTAL TIME: 45 MINUTES
PLUS COOLING

FOR THE CUPCAKES

240g self-raising flour

250g caster sugar

½ teaspoon bicarbonate of soda

1½ teaspoons ground cinnamon

1½ teaspoons ground ginger

¼ teaspoon ground cloves

270g unsalted butter, softened

4 large free-range eggs

3 tablespoons whole milk

1 tablespoon golden syrup

FOR THE BUTTERCREAM ICING

300g unsalted butter, softened

540g icing sugar

4 tablespoons brandy

YOU NEED

2 x 12-hole muffin trays,
with snug-fitting paper cases

Preheat the oven to 170°C fan/375°F/gas 5. Sift the dry cupcake ingredients and ¾ of a teaspoon of fine sea salt into a large bowl, add the butter and eggs, then beat for 60 seconds with an electric mixer (I prefer the free-standing type). Pour in the milk and golden syrup, then whisk for 20 seconds, or until well combined. Scrape down the sides of the bowl with a spatula, then give the mix a final blast for 30 seconds to make sure it's all incorporated. Fill the paper cases two-thirds full with mixture, but don't bother to smooth it out. Bake for 20 minutes, or until they spring back when touched. Leave to cool, transferring to a wire cooling rack after 5 minutes.

Meanwhile, make the icing. Beat the butter with an electric mixer for 4 to 5 minutes, or until pale and smooth. Sift the icing sugar into a large bowl, then add to the butter in two stages, beating well between each. Pour in the brandy and beat for a further 5 minutes, or until well combined – if the icing appears a little thick or you want more of a kick, add a splash more brandy. Once the cupcakes are cool, decorate them with a generous serving of the icing, then serve with a cup of eggnog while wearing a Santa hat – it's Christmas! I like to top these with lots of festive sprinkles too.

> Boozy and slightly spiced, these Christmas cupcakes are the perfect alternative to mince pies.

Mini Christmas puds

MAKES 48

TOTAL TIME: 35 MINUTES
PLUS COOLING

FOR THE PUDDINGS

140g plain flour

185g caster sugar

30g cocoa powder

½ teaspoon bicarbonate of soda

1 heaped teaspoon ground ginger

¼ teaspoon ground cloves

zest from ½ an unwaxed orange

1 large free-range egg

120ml coffee, cooled
(see tip page 112)

120ml buttermilk

110ml vegetable oil

FOR THE BUTTERCREAM ICING

150g unsalted butter, softened

270g icing sugar

2 tablespoons dark rum

YOU NEED

2 x 24-hole mini muffin trays,
with snug-fitting paper cases

1 x piping bag (with 5mm nozzle)

Preheat the oven to 160°C fan/350°F/gas 4. Sift the dry pudding ingredients and 1 pinch of fine sea salt into a large bowl, add the orange zest, then whisk with an electric mixer (I prefer the free-standing type) to combine. Mix the wet cupcake ingredients in a small bowl, then gradually add to the dry mix, whisking until silky smooth. Transfer the mixture to a small jug (you'll need to do this in batches) and carefully fill the paper cases two-thirds full. Bake for 10 minutes, or until they spring back when touched. Leave to cool, transferring to a wire cooling rack after 5 minutes.

Meanwhile, make the icing. Beat the butter with an electric mixer for 4 to 5 minutes, or until pale and smooth. Sift the icing sugar into another bowl, then add to the butter in two stages, beating well between each. Pour in the rum and beat for a further 5 minutes, or until well combined. Once the puds are cool, pipe them with the icing – with a bit of practice, you should be able to make them look like classic, albeit very mini, Christmas puddings – perfect.

> These are the perfect party treats – I like to top them with some holly and berry decorations to take them to another level.

Thanks for

I'm pretty amazed and overwhelmed that I've been given the chance to make this book, so the first person I'd like to thank is Jamie Oliver, who randomly remembered me one day and invited me to join his family of Food Tube merrymakers. You are genuinely one of the loveliest people I've ever met, and I really appreciate your honest enthusiasm for people doing what they love.

I'd also like to thank the amazing food team at Jamie Oliver HQ: Pip, Claire, Jenna and Joe, thank you for letting me get in the way, take over and wash up, even though you tried to stop me! Thanks for making my cupcakes look so brilliant. A special thanks also to the über-ace David Loftus for the beautiful photography in this book – I'm usually incredibly unphotogenic, so you're clearly very talented. You've all made this whole process so enjoyable and I'm super-grateful.

I would also like to thank the people behind the scenes – everyone at Superfantastic and Penguin, Rebecca, Malou, Caroline and Annie as well as my Food Tube family – without whom this book would not be in your hands right now, looking so brilliant!

A big thanks must go to my long-suffering mother. Mum, you've supported me unconditionally since I started making an absurd amount of mess in your kitchen. You've given me weather reports every market day, you've cleaned up after me, you've lent me your car, you've enveloped my exhausted body with hugs and love, and you've forgiven me when I've been too busy to see you. I love you and am so grateful for everything you've done for me since I popped out!

To my sister Holly, who, like Mum, has been the proudest, most supportive sister imaginable. The way you bombard friends and strangers with my story and exploits, you're like a walking, talking, free marketing tool! Thank you for being my counsellor, my friend and my favourite sister. I love you.

Thank you, Dad: you've supported every decision I've ever made (except that time I got my nose pierced, but let's not dwell on that!). You've always said your proudest father-daughter moment was when I told you I was dropping out of Camberwell College of Arts; you said you were proud that I was following my heart, so I have always tried to do that with everything in my life since. I am proud of how you have accepted your situation with grace and dignity. I love you very much.

Thanks must go to everyone who's helped so much at Crumbs & Doilies over the last few years – Cara, Emma, Maimie, Charlotte, Yui, Jerine, Roxie, B,

everything! *

Claudia, Phoebe, Greg, Grace, Natasha, Rachael, Laura M and Laura P – and to my current team of amazing girls – Sophie, Chanel, Francesca, Sally and Cat: you make me so proud! Your hard work, care and pride in your work are what makes C&D the success it is today. Many of the recipes in this book were developed with my team – so, readers, if you like these cakes, you have these girls to thank too. I'm particularly grateful to Sally, my right-hand woman: you drive the C&D train graciously, skilfully, humbly and tirelessly, and your dedication to both my and Sam's vision is priceless. Special thanks also goes to Cat, the engine-room controller, who manages the office and the orders as if she has three pairs of hands and three heads! Most importantly, you are my in-house therapist and my friend – I would be lost without you.

Thank you, Marisa, my best friend in the whole wide world. I know you asked me to thank you, because you want to see your name in a book, but I would have done it anyway, stoopid! You said recently that even after eating my cupcakes for nearly eight years, you are still surprised by how much you love them. Thank you for being the funniest person I know, the best friend I've ever had, the best customer (even though I give you free cakes!), the best person to do karaoke with and an all-round Brillo Pads woman! Thank

you also for marrying Phoebe, who is my second-favourite woman in the world. I love you both.

Lastly, I would like to thank Sam, my business partner, my ex-boyfriend, my friend. What a journey! Thank you for believing in me, for giving up your life to help me create this dream, for being so bloody smart and knowing EVERYTHING all the time! Thanks for wanting me to be the best I can be, for forgiving me when I failed at that, for pushing me, even though it hurt sometimes, for being an innovator and an unlikely cake-mastermind. I definitely would not be doing what I'm doing if it wasn't for you. Thank you for helping me with this book and for being my partner.

PENGUIN BOOKS

Published by the Penguin Group

Penguin Books Ltd,
80 Strand,
London WC2R 0RL, England

Penguin Group (USA) Inc.
375 Hudson Street,
New York, New York 10014, USA

Penguin Group (Canada),
90 Eglinton Avenue East, Suite 700,
Toronto, Ontario, Canada M4P 2Y3
(a division of Pearson Penguin Canada Inc.)

Penguin Ireland,
25 St Stephen's Green,
Dublin 2, Ireland
(a division of Penguin Books Ltd)

Penguin Group (Australia),
707 Collins Street,
Melbourne, Victoria 3008, Australia
(a division of Pearson Australia Group Pty Ltd)

Penguin Books India Pvt Ltd,
11 Community Centre,
Panchsheel Park, New Delhi – 110 017, India

Penguin Group (NZ),
67 Apollo Drive,
Rosedale, Auckland 0632, New Zealand
(a division of Pearson New Zealand Ltd)

Penguin Books (South Africa) (Pty) Ltd,
Block D, Rosebank Office Park,
181 Jan Smuts Avenue, Parktown North,
Gauteng 2193, South Africa

Penguin Books Ltd, Registered Offices:
80 Strand, London WC2R 0RL, England

First published 2014
003

Copyright © Jemma Wilson, 2014
Photography © Jamie Oliver Enterprises Limited, 2014

Jamie Oliver is a registered trade mark

is registered as copyright
with the Library of Congress
© Jamie Oliver Enterprises, 2013

Jamie Oliver's Food Tube is produced by
Fresh One Productions Limited

Photography by David Loftus

Design by Superfantastic

Printed in Italy
Colour reproduction by Altaimage Ltd

ISBN: 978-0-718-17920-5

www.penguin.co.uk
www.jamieoliver.com
www.youtube.com/jamieoliver
www.freshone.tv

CHECK OUT THE OTHER TITLES IN THIS SERIES: